Paddling & Hiking Ontario's Southern Shield Country

Paddling & Hiking Ontario's Southern Shield Country

KAS STONE

The BOSTON
MILLS PRESS

A BOSTON MILLS PRESS BOOK

LIBRARY AND ARCHIVES CANADA CATALOGUING
IN PUBLICATION

Stone, Kas
Paddling and hiking Ontario's southern shield
country / Kas Stone.

Includes bibliographical references and index.
ISBN 1-55046-437-X

1. Hiking--Ontario--Guidebooks.
2. Trails--Ontario--Guidebooks.
3. Canoes and canoeing--Ontario--Guidebooks.
4. Ontario--Guidebooks. I. Title.

GV199.44.C22058 2005   796.51'09713
C2004-906377-4

PUBLISHER CATALOGING-IN-PUBLICATION DATA
(U.S.)

Stone, Kathleen Ann
Paddling and hiking Ontario's southern shield
country / Kas Stone. . _ 1st ed.
[176] p. : col. photos., maps ; cm.
Includes index.
Summary: The single-day excursions in this
book explore the southern part of Ontario's
rugged shield country, and most combine hiking
and paddling in roughly equal measure.
ISBN 1-55046-437-X (pbk.)
1. Canoes and canoeing _ Ontario _ Guidebooks.
2. Hiking -- Ontario _ Guidebooks.
3. Ontario _ Guidebooks. I. Title.
797.122'09713 22   GV776.15.O57.S766
2005

PUBLISHED BY BOSTON MILLS PRESS
132 Main Street, Erin, Ontario
Canada N0B 1T0
Tel 519-833-2407   Fax 519-833-2195
e-mail: books@bostonmillspress.com
www.bostonmillspress.com

IN CANADA:
Distributed by Firefly Books Ltd.
66 Leek Crescent, Richmond Hill, Ontario
Canada L4B 1H1

IN THE UNITED STATES:
Distributed by Firefly Books (U.S.) Inc.
P.O. Box 1338, Ellicott Station
Buffalo, New York, USA 14205

The publisher acknowledges for the financial
support of our publishing program the Canada
Council, the Ontario Arts Council, and the
Government of Canada through the Book
Publishing Industry Development Program
(BPIDP).

All photographs by Kas Stone unless
otherwise noted.

Maps by Kas Stone

Text and cover design by
Sue Breen and Chris McCorkindale
McCorkindale Advertising & Design

Printed in Canada

Contents

What This Book Is About   9
Measurements and Conversions   11
Maps Legend   11

Introduction to Ontario's Shield
Physical Landscape   13
Natural Inhabitants   16
Human Inhabitants   19

1: Frontenac   23
Frontenac's Southern Highlands   25

2: Bon Echo   33
Mazinaw–Kishkebus Loop   36
Petroglyphs and Pictographs   42

3: Achray   47
Barron Canyon   48
Berm Lake and High Falls   51
Pine Trees of Ontario's Shield   57

4: Silent Lake   63
Silent Lake and Bonnie's Pond   66

5: Petroglyphs   73
Eels Creek and the Petroglyphs   74

6: Algonquin's Highway 60 Corridor   81
Rock Lake and Booth's Rock   84
Madawaska River and Centennial Ridges   88
Cache Lake and Track & Tower Trail   92

7: The Frost Centre   101
Raven Lake and the Geomorphology Hike   103

8: The Massasauga — 115
Blackstone Harbour and Baker Trail — 118
Georgian Bay and Wreck Island — 120

9: Grundy — 127
Gut Lake to Pakeshkag Lake — 128

10: Killarney — 135
George-Freeland Lakes and "The Crack" — 137
Bell Lake and Silver Peak — 141
Chikanishing River and Georgian Bay Coast — 145
Acid Rain in Killarney — 152

11: Mississagi — 155
Flack Lake and Old Baldy — 156
Semiwite–Helenbar Lakes and McKenzie Trail — 159

12: A Taste of Superior — 165
Agawa's Rocks — 168
Bald Head and Orphan Lake — 174
Gargantua's Bays, Capes and Islands — 177
Old Woman Bay and Brûlé Harbour — 183

Appendix I: Gear for Paddling & Hiking Excursions — 193

Appendix II: Excursions with Your Dog — 203

Appendix III: Useful Contacts — 207

Index — 208

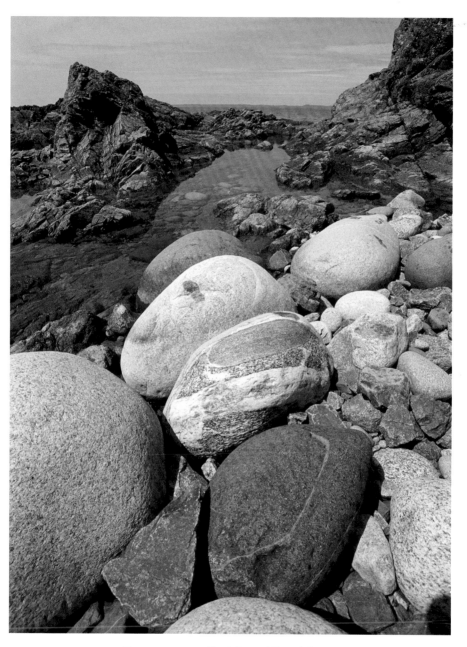

For my parents, Patricia and David Stone,
who passed on to me their love of hiking, paddling and the wild outdoors,
and who have been so supportive in the writing of this book.

What This Book Is About

This book contains a collection of excursions that explore, both on foot and by kayak or canoe, the portion of the Canadian Shield that lies within southern Ontario. It is a practical guide that includes detailed descriptions of twenty-two paddling and hiking excursions together with route maps, photographs and information about where to stay and what to see, as well as useful contacts in the excursion areas. It points out interesting features along the routes and discusses the natural and human historical context of those features. *Paddling & Hiking* also celebrates the wild beauty and variety of the Shield landscape. Its excursions scramble to heights of land to admire the splendid views, drift along the shorelines of winding rivers and rocky lakes to enjoy their peaceful solitude, and venture to remote islands to appreciate their windswept isolation.

The Canadian Shield is the core of the North American continent. In Ontario it stretches from the Rideau River and the St. Lawrence River in the southeast, across the Highlands of Addington, the Kawarthas, Algonquin and Haliburton, around the Muskoka Lakes and Georgian Bay's 30,000 Islands, through Algoma's Rainbow Country and into the vast northern wilderness beyond Lake Superior. Past the Ontario border, the Shield extends northeast into Quebec, northwest into Manitoba, and in the far north into Nunavut and the Northwest Territories. The excursions described here explore the southern part of Ontario's Shield – the part that is within easy reach of the province's large population centres and that is known affectionately as "cottage country." Each chapter contains one or more excursions set in the same location. Many excursions are found within national or provincial parks or Crown preserves, whose boundaries afford protection for much of Ontario's remaining Shield wilderness and whose campsites offer excellent bases for exploring that wilderness. The excursions are organized geographically from southeast to northwest.

Every excursion presented here includes both hiking and paddling segments, so that features along the route can be appreciated from the perspective of both land and water. The two perspectives can be remarkably different – sometimes more intimate, sometimes more comprehensive, and often more appropriate from one viewpoint than from the other. A spectacular clifftop lookout can become a mere bump on the shoreline when seen from the cockpit of a kayak, and a bog impassable for the hiker can become a fascinating exploration of marshland plants and animals from the seat of a canoe. Most of the excursions combine hiking and paddling in

Brûlé Harbour shoreline, Lake Superior

1	Frontenac	7	The Frost Centre Lands
2	Bon Echo	8	The Massasauga
3	Achray	9	Grundy
4	Silent Lake	10	Killarney
5	Petroglyphs	11	Mississagi
6	Algonquin's Hwy 60 Corridor	12	Lake Superior

roughly equal measure. In some excursions, however, the paddling portion of the route serves merely to give access to an otherwise remote trail, and in others the hike is merely a brief leg-stretch to break a lengthy paddle.

The excursions are intended to be day-trips — excursions that a reasonably fit person with basic competence in paddling and hiking can comfortably accomplish in a single day. The paddling is entirely flat-water, with only an occasional gentle current to navigate, and the portages are infrequent and usually short. The hiking trails are often rugged but none require any technical climbing skills or equipment apart from a reliable pair of comfortable hiking boots. Some of the routes are circular, others linear, but they all return to the starting point so car-shuttling is not needed. Alternative routes are frequently suggested, in order to accommodate differing levels of physical ability and available time. None of the routes should be undertaken lightly, however, as the Shield terrain is inherently rough and the routes across it can be strenuous.

Distances in this book are referred to using metric measurements. Many have been rounded to the nearest 100 m or 0.5 km, according to the context, as the intent is to give general guidance with reasonable accuracy rather than exact distances with pinpoint precision. To avoid disrupting the flow of the text, alternative measurements (miles, yards and acres) have not been included parenthetically after each reference. The following table may be used to convert the metric measurements.

Measurements and Conversions		
1 kilometre (km)	=	0.62 miles (mi)
1 metre (m)	=	3.25 feet (ft)
1 metre (m)	=	1.1 yard (yd)
1 square kilometre (km²)	=	100 hectares (ha)
1 square kilometre (km²)	=	10,000 acres (ac)

Each excursion is accompanied by a map showing the excursion route, alternative routes, access points, campsites, lookouts and other features along the way. References in the text to locations on the map are indicated by bold red letters. Most of the chapters that describe more than one excursion also include an index map to show the excursions' locations relative to each other.

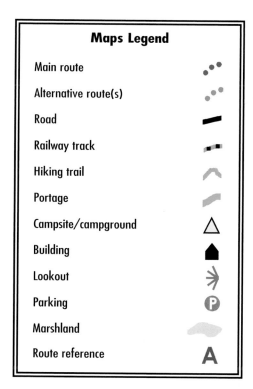

Maps Legend	
Main route	
Alternative route(s)	
Road	
Railway track	
Hiking trail	
Portage	
Campsite/campground	
Building	
Lookout	
Parking	
Marshland	
Route reference	A

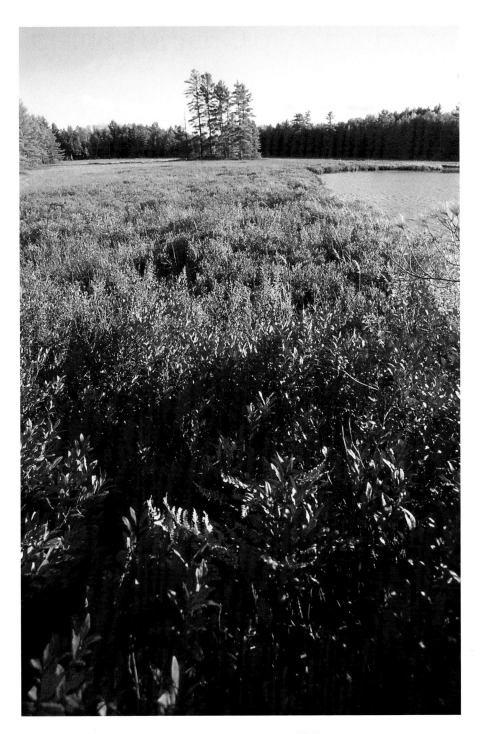

Fall colours at Clutes Lake, Bon Echo

Introduction to Ontario's Shield

Physical Landscape

The Canadian Shield is not an extravagant landscape. It has no jagged mountain peaks or breathtaking valleys; its highlands are only a few metres higher than its lowlands. It has no dramatic Fundy tides or Niagara gorges, no arctic ice-fields or prairie wheat-fields stretching into infinity. The Shield's beauty is of a subtler sort. It is a landscape of undulating rock interspersed with patchy soil and boggy wetlands, populated by windblown pines and scraggly spruce, cattails and cottongrass, bullfrogs and beavers.

The landscape of the Canadian Shield is the product of its geological past. Some of Ontario's rocks are extremely ancient, so the province's geological history is long and complex. The story begins between 3.5 and 2.5 billion years ago when a collection of small continents, volcanic islands and sedimentary debris on the ocean floor were pushed together by plate tectonic forces to form the foundation of a continent that became North America. This part of Ontario's Shield, which encompasses the area north of Lake Superior from Sault Ste. Marie to the Manitoba border, is called the Superior Province. In this book only the excursions at Lake Superior Provincial Park (Chapter 12) are located in the Superior Province.

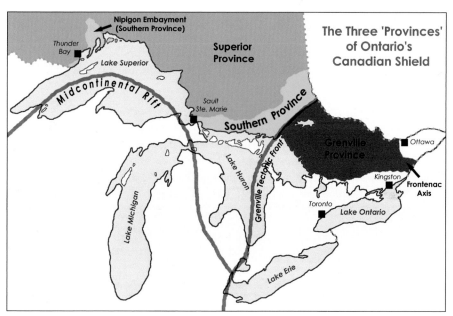

The next major period of geological activity in the Shield, from 2.5 to 2 billion years ago, was the extensive erosion of Superior Province rocks to form deep beds of sediment, followed by the compressing and uplifting of those sediments to form a massive mountain range on the southern edge of the Superior Province — called, consequently, the Southern Province. Only a small band of the Southern Province is found in Canada, lying across the northern shore of Lake Huron and Georgian Bay, where this book's excursions in Killarney and Mississagi provincial parks (chapters 10 and 11) are located, and in the Nipigon area beyond the range of this book. The bulk of the Southern Province stretches southeast into the states of Michigan, Minnesota and Wisconsin.

Cottongrass on the Chikanishing Trail, Killarney

Between 2 and 1 billion years ago, the final piece was added to Ontario's Shield — a patchwork of small chunks of continental crust that collided with each other and rammed into the southern edge of the Southern Province to form another mountain range. This section of the Shield, the Grenville Province, extends southeastward from Georgian Bay across the Highlands of Haliburton, Algonquin, Kawartha and Addington, tapering just north of Kingston to a finger called the Frontenac Axis. Most of the excursions in this book are within the Grenville Province.

The ancient bedrock of the Canadian Shield is predominantly metamorphic, its rocks formed by the squeezing and heating of pre-existing rocks, which changed them chemically and structurally from their original form. Some of the Shield's original rocks were sedimentary. The quartz-rich sediments that washed off the Superior Province, for instance, were metamorphosed into the brilliant white quartzite found in Killarney and Mississagi today, and the beds of limestone laid down in primeval seas in the southeast were metamorphosed into the marble seen in Frontenac Park. Other original rocks were igneous. The igneous granite that solidified from magma deep within the Earth was transformed into gneiss (pronounced "nice"), a metamorphic rock found commonly across the entire Shield. The igneous rock that solidified from lava that erupted onto the Earth's surface was transformed into metamorphic rocks like greenstone, found along Lake Superior's northern shore, and amphibolite, found in pockets in the Grenville Province. Still others of the original rocks were already metamorphic, becoming increasingly deformed with each episode of compression and heating.

To further complicate the geologic mix, shifts in the Earth's crust at various times throughout its history fractured the ancient bedrock, allowing magma to ooze upward and fill the gaps with intrusions of igneous rock — plutons (large subterranean bubbles) of granite, beds of basalt, and dikes and sills (vertical and horizontal bands respectively) of diabase. The most significant of these crustal shifts, just over 1 billion years ago, resulted in the formation of a 2,000 km crescent-shaped fracture called the Midcontinental Rift underlying present-day Lake Superior and created many cliffs, dikes and sills along the Lake Superior coast. The crustal shifting that pushed the Grenville Province against the Southern Province 2 to 1.5 billion years ago created an enormous pluton along the Grenville Tectonic Front, which later became the spectacular red granite of Killarney Park. And the successive collisions that welded together the various segments of the Grenville Province produced the extraordinary ribbons of rock seen in modern road-cuts all across cottage country, and quite spectacularly along the highway south of Parry Sound.

Diabase ribbons on the Lake Superior shoreline

Complex rock formations in a Parry Sound road-cut

15

The most recent chapter in the geological history of Ontario's Shield has been the scouring and levelling of its terrain by glaciation. More than twenty times in the last 2.5 million years, during extended periods of atmospheric coolness, sheets of ice up to 3 km thick advanced southward across the land, grinding away the ancient mountain ranges and carrying rocky debris great distances. During inter-glacial periods of relative warmth when the ice retreated northward, the meltwater produced tremendous rivers and vast lakes that washed tons of sediment off the Shield, and deposited it in thick beds across southern Ontario and the northeastern United States.

The last glacier, the Laurentide Ice Sheet, reached its maximum extent about 20,000 years ago, pushing well south of the Ontario border. It retreated between 13,000 and 10,000 years ago, exposing the undulating landscape of twisted bedrock and patchy soil that makes up Ontario's Shield today.

Natural Inhabitants

In the 10,000 years since the Laurentide Ice Sheet retreated, the Shield has become home to a hardy assortment of flora and fauna. They have managed to adapt, both to the rugged geology and to the short summers and harsh winters that are characteristic of the mid-latitude climate.

Deciduous forest on La Cloche Silhouette Trail, Killarney

Coniferous forest on the Lakeshore Trail, the Frost Centre

Ontario's southern Shield lies within the Great Lakes–St. Lawrence vegetation region, a transition zone between the Carolinian deciduous forest region of the south and the coniferous boreal forest of the north. It contains a mixture of trees, shrubs and flowers from both regions, many of them at the northerly or southerly limits of their tolerance.

The Shield's deciduous trees have broad leaves that are grown each year for the purpose of photosynthesis (the process by which trees utilize water, carbon dioxide, sunlight and chlorophyll to produce the carbohydrate energy they need to live). They shed these leaves at the end of the growing season every autumn. Deciduous trees also produce an annual crop of seeds, which can take the form of fruit, nuts, catkins or winged keys. The seasonal cycle of leaf growth and seed production requires abundant nourishment and an extended period of warmth and light, so deciduous trees need relatively deep, rich soil and are best suited to the longer growing seasons in the southern part of the Shield and the protection of south-facing hillside slopes. Each deciduous tree has a niche within the environment. The "pioneer" species like birch, poplar and aspen quickly colonize open areas that have been disturbed by fire or logging. Sun-loving trees like red oak perch on dry hilltops. And in areas of deep, well-drained soil, several species of maple make their homes, including the sugar maple, famous for its sweet syrup and its blazing autumn colours.

The Shield's coniferous trees have needles rather than leaves, which they typically retain for several years, giving them an "evergreen" appearance. Their seeds are housed within scaly cones, which for some conifers take several seasons to develop. The extraordinary jack pine has been known to keep its cones for as long as 25 years awaiting ideal growing conditions. These features give northern-dwelling conifers two distinct advantages over their deciduous cousins. First, because they do not produce a full annual crop of leaves or seeds, they do not have the same energy requirements as deciduous trees and are able to survive in impoverished soil. Second, they are able to begin photosynthesis immediately in the spring and take maximum advantage of the year's available sunlight.

The Shield's conifers, like its deciduous trees, have adapted to specialized niches within the environment, and are typically found growing in scant soil on clifftops and headlands, or along the saturated edges of wetlands and river valleys. Common among them are the three species of pine (see *Pine Trees of Ontario's Shield*, page 57), the ubiquitous balsam fir, the scraggly black spruce, its more presentable sibling the white spruce, the unusual tamarack that sheds its needles every fall, and the hemlock and cedar, which are both at the northern limits of their range in the Shield.

On a smaller scale, the wildflowers of the Shield are a diverse and enterprising bunch. They burst forth in early spring in deciduous forests before the leafy canopy closes over and plunges the forest floor into darkness. A few shade-tolerant species thrive in the shadows. Most wildflowers, however, spend the summer jostling for sunshine on patches of open ground — barren cliffs and hilltops, burnout areas left by forest fires, clearcut swaths left by logging, and peripheral regions around wetlands and rivers. Most unusual among the wetland plants are the carnivorous pitcher plants and sundews, which compensate for the lack of nutrients in the saturated soil by catching and digesting insects.

Insects are perhaps the most conspicuous inhabitants of Ontario's Shield, the bountiful bug population — from the first crops of blackflies and mosquitoes in mid-May to the deerflies and horseflies of summer — accompanying hikers and paddlers on their excursions. Though they can be an irritant to humans, these insects provide a welcome feast for many species of birds, fish, reptiles and amphibians, which are plentiful across the Shield. More elusive is the mammal population. While the Shield is home to several species of wild canines, hoofed mammals, a healthy number of black bears and a great many members of the rodent and weasel families, they are naturally suspicious of people and are therefore rarely seen. Mounds of scat and tracks on the hiking trails are often the only evidence of their presence.

Boreal forest in the Stag Lake Peatland, Mississagi

The fortifications of industrious beavers are conspicuous throughout the Shield, their dams profoundly altering the wetland landscape. From the beavers' perspective the dams create lakes out of rivers so that they can build lodges with underwater entrances to protect their families from predators and from winter's icy chill. Their luxurious pelts were in great demand in the fashion markets of seventeenth and eighteenth century Europe, and supported the thriving fur trade that opened Ontario's Shield to exploration and eventually to settlement.

Human Inhabitants

Archeological evidence suggests that at the height of the last period of glaciation 20,000 years ago, so much water was bound up in ice sheets that ocean levels were significantly lowered and a corridor of land was exposed between Asia and Alaska. Across this corridor came several species of large mammals and, in pursuit, the first humans on this continent — the Paleo-Indians, who became the indigenous people of North America. As the glaciers retreated between 13,000 and 10,000 years ago, the Bering Sea closed over the land corridor, Ontario's Shield was gradually uncovered, and these "Native" people moved into it. The earliest inhabitants were people of the Plano culture who lived as migratory hunters armed with primitive stone tools, following the herds of roving animals. Gradually, during the periods of the Woodland and Laurel Native cultures between 5,000 BC and AD 500, increasingly sophisticated tools were developed and an increasingly diverse society emerged that included fishing, agriculture and maple syrup production. From these ancestors came the Algonkian-speaking tribes of recent times — the Cree of the northwestern Shield, the Ojibwe of the northeast, and the Odawa and Algonquins in the south and east.

The seasonal customs of Native life were abruptly altered in the seventeenth century when Europeans ventured across Ontario's Shield in search of a route to the riches of silk and spice in the Far East. When North America proved too great an obstacle, they began to focus on the potential riches of the newfound continent itself.

The first of these riches was fur — beaver for the hats of fashionable gentlemen, and other stylish pelts like lynx and ermine to adorn collars and cuffs. For two centuries from the mid-1600s to the mid-1800s, Ontario's Shield bustled with birchbark canoes: the small canoes (popularly known in the French fur trade as the *canot du nord*) that Native and European trappers used to gather pelts along the interior waterways and take them to trading posts; and the large canoes used by *voyageurs* on the

Great Lakes and larger rivers to transport pelts from trading posts to the major ports for shipment to Europe, and to bring European trade-goods (most notably cloth, household implements, weapons and alcohol) in return. During this era the Shield also bristled with competition. The French and their network of Native allies collected furs for the Northwest Company and dominated the waters draining eastward into the St. Lawrence River toward the port of Montreal. The English and their Hudson's Bay Company traded furs and controlled the northern lands around James Bay and Hudson Bay. The 1763 Treaty of Paris between England and France ceded France's territory in North America to the English, stopping (officially at least!) the conflict between the nations. With the merger of the Hudson's Bay Company and the Northwest Company in 1821 the commercial competition also ended. And the entire contest became irrelevant by the mid-1800s, as the dwindling supply of fur and changing fashions in Europe led to the abandonment of the fur trade.

Industrialization transformed Europe and the United States in the 1800s, and attention turned again to Ontario's Shield, where a wealth of raw materials still lay. Logging became the main human activity across the Shield as the nineteenth century unfolded. Great forests of white and red pine fell to the axe during the winter months, to be sent in the spring on swollen rivers to mills and ports downstream. The lumber was then shipped to England to supply the British navy with masts, and to America for the construction of its burgeoning cities. Lesser species like fir, hemlock and spruce became the fence posts of the nation and the ties supporting the ribbons of railway that wound westward across the continent. Toward the end of the century a use was even found for the lowly black spruce, when increasingly widespread literacy prompted the development of cheaper means for producing paper and launched the pulp and paper industry. Logging of timber and pulpwood continues today, though its extent and methods are subject to environmental controls that were not considered necessary a century ago, when forest resources must have seemed inexhaustible.

Mining became another mainstay of the Shield economy during the industrial period. The complex geological history of the Shield left large deposits of commercially useful base metals (copper, zinc, nickel and iron) and an enormous supply of aggregate for road construction. It also created pockets of valuable minerals, such as the gold at Hemlo and the silver at Silver Islet, and gemstones like amethyst near Thunder Bay and garnet, sodalite and corundum in the Bancroft area.

Fishing has been part of the Shield's economy for many centuries. Native people harvested lake trout and whitefish in abundance during their seasonal migrations. In the nineteenth and early twentieth centuries a commercial fishery thrived in the Great Lakes, until contamination, overfishing and competition from foreign interlopers (the sea lamprey in the mid-1900s being a prime culprit) decimated fish populations. A small commercial fishery remains, but in recent decades fishing on the Shield has become largely recreational, as sports fishermen and cottage-goers angle for any species, native or invader, that will take the hook.

Until the twentieth century, permanent settlement was sparse across Ontario's Shield. The Shield's remoteness and rough topography made transportation routes difficult to establish and costly to maintain, and in the absence of adequate transportation, settlement was sluggish. Logging gradually opened the Shield to primitive road travel during the mid-1800s, and the invention of the steam-powered engine prompted the development of the country's railway system in the latter part of the century. Small communities and farms grew up along these transportation routes to provide food and services for the people employed in the lumber and mining industries (and in road and railway construction) but many were abandoned as the timber and mineral resources became depleted and the workers moved on.

Then in the twentieth century an increasingly affluent population, stressed by urban life and blessed with the automobile, discovered the recreation potential of the Shield. Cottages sprang up like mushrooms from the land around the lakes, marinas launched fleets of pleasure-boats, towns blossomed at crossroads to serve the needs of travellers, and the era of the cottage country summer weekend commute began.

Modern highways cut across the landscape today, making the Shield accessible. As we whiz down the tarmac, it is easy to underestimate the ruggedness of the terrain and to forget that, not so long ago, it was a vast unbroken wilderness through which only a few hardy travellers made their way on foot and by canoe. Although some of the Shield's original character has been lost to development, significant pockets of wilderness still remain. And in these pockets we can still make our way, on foot and by canoe or kayak, and experience the wonders of the Shield — the view from a clifftop lookout, the ripple of water off the paddle, the smell of pine needles as they crunch underfoot, the cry of the loon and the cackle of ravens, the sun and wind on our faces, and the blissful tiredness that comes at the end of a day spent hiking and paddling.

Chapter 1

Frontenac

Overview

Frontenac Provincial Park is located in southeastern Ontario about 50 km north of Kingston. It is a large, natural-environment park in which "development" has been confined to an excellent system of hiking trails, portages, and backcountry campsites, and most of the parkland is off-limits to motorized vehicles and motorboats. With 170 km of trails and 29 lakes, it is a paradise for the hiker, paddler and nature lover.

Geologically, Frontenac Park is situated on top of a finger of ancient bedrock — the Frontenac Axis — which connects the Grenville Province of the Canadian Shield in the northwest with the Adirondack Mountains to the southeast. Local variations in the bedrock give the landscape of Frontenac its splendid diversity. In the northern part of the park, where the bedrock is predominantly soft lime-rich marble, glaciers have eroded a lowland and filled it with comparatively thick fertile soil. This foundation supports a great variety of vegetation, including tall, deciduous trees and some unusual ferns and orchids. In the southern part of the park, by contrast, the bedrock began life as a pluton, a bubble of magma that pushed upward from deep inside the Earth's crust and solidified to form a highland of erosion-resistant rock called diorite. Glaciation scoured its surface, leaving only thin pockets of soil to sustain hardy types of vegetation. Three fires in the nineteenth and twentieth centuries further hampered plant growth. And poor drainage created a network of acidic ponds and extensive marshlands between the ridges of exposed rock. So the landscape of the south is bleak and rugged, with much open space and many lovely vistas. Between north and south is a transitional zone of bedrock that supports, as one might expect, a transitional type of landscape with rocky outcrops and wooded glens. The route described here begins and ends in the transitional zone but takes in a large area of the southern zone en route.

Of the many animal species that inhabit Frontenac Park, undoubtedly its most interesting is the black rat snake. Frontenac is one of only five isolated pockets of wilderness in Ontario where this reptile can be found. It is classified as "threatened," and its remaining population is protected under provincial wildlife law. The black rat snake is Canada's largest snake,

Slide Lake (photo by David Stone)

reaching a length of up to two metres. Adults are shiny black-brown along the back, with creamy throats and grey bellies, often with a checkerboard pattern or blotches of brown, orange or red. They are constrictors, killing their prey, typically small mammals and birds, with suffocating coils. They are also semi-arboreal, equally at home in trees as on the ground, so nestlings and eggs make up a significant portion of their diet. Their preferred habitat is along the borders of deciduous woodlands adjacent to old fields. It is rare, but thrilling, to come across a black rat snake along the trail. Much more common are the ubiquitous garter snake and the feisty northern water snake.

Access

- From Hwy 401 at Kingston, take exit #613.
- Drive north on County Road 9 to its end.
- Turn left onto County Road 5 (Rutledge Road).
- Turn right after about 2 km, and follow the park signs through Sydenham onto County Road 19 (Bedford Road).
- After about 10 km (which feels like 20 because it's so twisty!), turn right onto Salmon Lake Road.
- Stop at the Trail Centre just inside the park entrance and buy a permit.
- Drive to the end of Salmon Lake Road, where there is a boat launch and a car parking area.

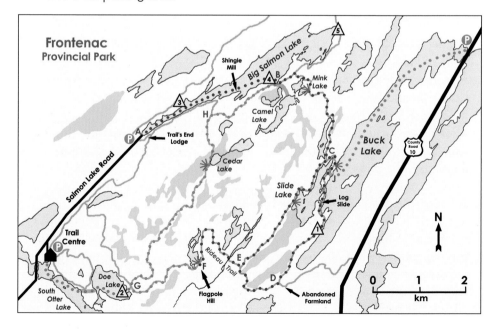

The route outlined here is long and strenuous — a total of 6 km of paddling and 20 km of hiking over very rugged terrain. To complete it in a single day requires an early start and a full day at an energetic pace. Slightly shorter routes are possible, or the excursion can be tackled in a more leisurely way by breaking it into two days and camping in the park.

• Main Route: 20 km hike, 6 km paddle
• Alternative(s): 8 – 22 km hike, 4 – 8 km paddle, 0 – 682 m portage(s)

Route Description
1st Segment: Big Salmon Lake launch to Camel Lake Portage (3 km paddle)
From the launch A, paddle along the southern shoreline of Big Salmon Lake. Today little evidence of human presence remains here. But in the late 1800s, during the height of logging activity in the area when Big Salmon Lake was a marshalling place for logs being driven to Bedford Mills, a shingle mill operated on a point about 2 km from the launch. And in 1947 the Trail's End Lodge was built on the small hill just east of the launch. Until its closure in the mid-1960s, the lodge served as a base for sport fishermen. Two-thirds of the way along Big Salmon Lake, just past campsite cluster #4, there is a small sandy beach B at the start of the Camel Lake portage, where your kayak or canoe can be left during the hike that follows.

2nd Segment: Camel Lake Portage to Slide Lake Junction via Mink Lake Trail (3.5 km hike)
A short distance up the Camel Lake portage, turn left onto the Big Salmon Lake trail and follow it about 3.5 km to the start of the Mink Lake trail, which exits to the right. It climbs over open, rocky ground to the panoramic Mink Lake Lookout, then winds southward along ridges of exposed bedrock and into steep ravines beside ribbon-like lakes to the northern junction of the Slide Lake trail C.

3rd Segment: Slide Lake East Side (3.5 km hike)
Turn left at the junction onto the Slide Lake trail. It curves around the north end of Slide Lake, then continues south down the thin ridge of land that separates Slide Lake from Buck Lake. Slide Lake gets its name from the logging slideway that used to cross this ridge, about half way down the lake, carrying timber from the interior to lumber mills on larger rivers outside the park area. The trail visits a lookout over Buck Lake, then passes campsite cluster #1, and edges around a marshland where heron nests

Flagpole Hill

can be seen perched in the branches of dead trees. Finally it emerges into a surprisingly lush field, a remnant of farmland that was worked in the area between the mid-1800s and mid-1900s, and reaches a trail junction **D**.

4th Segment: Rideau Trail from Slide Lake to Flagpole Hill (3.5 km) and back (2.2 km hike)

At the junction, turn right onto the Rideau Trail, which runs through the southern end of Frontenac Park on its way from Kingston to Ottawa. The trail soon comes to another junction **E**, where the weary can turn right and begin the homeward trek (this shortens the hike by about 4.5 km but leaves out one of its highlights). Otherwise, continuing on, the path snakes over rough terrain, crossing many barren outcrops and skirting small boggy lakes before climbing to a commanding lookout over the southern end of the park at Flagpole Hill **F**. This makes an excellent place for a picnic lunch before you turn back. Retrace the route to the southwestern Slide Lake trail junction **E** and turn left.

5th Segment: Slide Lake West Side (3.5 km hike)

Edging around an impressive wetland, the trail arrives at the southern end of Slide Lake atop an enormous rock, where a signpost reads, appropriately, "A bloody great rock by a bonnie wee loch." The walk along the west side of Slide Lake takes you over high, open ground with smooth rocks sliding steeply into the water and lovely views over the lake.

6th Segment: Homeward (3.5 km hike, 3 km paddle)

Upon reaching the trail junction C at the northern end of Slide Lake, turn left onto the Mink Lake trail and retrace the route to your boat. If you still have time and energy before the final homeward leg to the launch, the eastern end of Big Salmon Lake, with its sprinkling of pretty islands, is well worth exploring.

Alternative 1: Slide Lake — Cedar Lake Loop (22 km hike, 6 km paddle)

This route extends the hike slightly and turns it into a full circle loop of 22 km. At the bottom of the Mink Lake Trail C, turn right instead of left onto the Slide Lake trail. Follow the trail along the west side of Slide Lake and turn right again at the Slide Lake southern junction E. Continue past Flagpole Hill F to Doe Lake near campsite #2 G. Turn right onto the Cedar Lake trail and follow it northward. This portion of the route is gentler underfoot and passes through forests of oak, maple and birch. The trail also takes in an impressive wetland near Cedar Lake, which it crosses by means of a long boardwalk. At the end of the Cedar Lake trail H turn right onto the Big Salmon Lake trail for the final 1.7 km stretch to your boat.

Alternative 2: Buck Lake Access (8.2 km hike, 8 km paddle, 16 m portages)

Launch from the Buck Lake access point where County Road 10 crosses the northern end of the lake. Paddle southwest 4 km to the portage into

Slide Lake (photo by David Stone)

Mink Lake lookout (photo by David Stone)

Slide Lake J and leave your boat pulled ashore there. Join the Slide Lake trail for the loop around the lake. If time permits, take the short portage (8 m) into Slide Lake and explore it from the water, then return over the portage and up Buck Lake to the launch. This approach cuts the hiking portion to slightly less than half the length of the main route and extends the paddling portion by about 2 km. Note that Buck Lake is a large and possibly windy lake. It is also dotted with private cottages and can be busy with motorboat traffic. Slide Lake, by comparison, is blissfully quiet; its only buildings are the remains of a couple of primitive cabins from the mid-1900s.

Alternative 3: Trail Centre Access (16.5 to 21 km hike, 4 km paddle, 68 m portages)

To approach the trail from the opposite end with just a short paddle each way, launch your boat from the Trail Centre into South Otter Lake, portage into Doe Lake, join the trail system at campsite cluster #2 G and either head north on the Cedar Lake trail to hike the entire Cedar–Mink–Slide Lake loop (21 km), or turn east over Flagpole Hill to hike the Slide Lake loop and back again over Flagpole Hill (16.5 km).

Other Paddling & Hiking Opportunities

The excursion and alternatives described in this chapter cover the southern half of Frontenac Park fairly comprehensively. The northern half of the park, with its more luxuriant landscape and its gentler character, has many trails and lakes to explore and several possible access points for hiking and paddling excursions. Also, two short trails begin at the park's Trail Centre. The first, the Arab Lake Trail (1 km), follows the Arab Lake Gorge and has a series of numbered posts corresponding to entries in the trail's interpretive guide, which describes the ecology and geology of the area. The second, the Doe Lake Trail (3 km), follows the South Otter Lake shoreline, crosses to a lookout over Doe Lake, and then loops back past a marshland to the Trail Centre. With its wealth of trails and lakes, Frontenac has tremendous scope for hiking and paddling. So buy a map and plot your own excursion!

Just outside Frontenac Provincial Park there are also many other opportunities for hiking and paddling:

- The Rideau Trail is a hiking trail that runs for 387 km between Kingston and Ottawa, passing through Frontenac Park along the way. Many sections of this trail are worth hiking while you're in the Frontenac area. A guidebook with detailed maps is available from the Rideau Trail Association. For information contact the association at (613) 545-0823, www.ncf.ca/rta.

- The Rideau Waterway, a series of connected lakes, rivers and canals stretching 202 km from Kingston to Ottawa, offers lots of opportunities for the paddler, although much of the route is shared with motorcraft. For information, nautical charts and guidebooks contact the Friends of the Rideau at (613) 283-5810, www.rideaufriends.com. The Rideau Waterway is also home to the Canadian Recreational Canoeing Association, which may be contacted in Merrickville at (613) 269-2910, www.crca.ca.

- The Gould Lake Conservation Area is a day-use park just north of Sydenham. It has 20 km of hiking trails inside the park and access to the Rideau Trail for longer hikes, paddling in Gould Lake, a beach, a grassy picnic area, toilets and parking. For information contact (613) 546-4228, www.cataraquiregion.on.ca/lands/gould.htm.

- Foley Mountain Conservation Area is a day-use park located on the north side of Westport. It is situated along a geological fault, which has given it a spectacular cliff overlooking Upper Rideau Lake. There is an extensive system of hiking trails in the park and access to the Rideau Trail. There is also a beach for swimming and access to

29

Marshland along the trail from Mink Lake to Slide Lake (photo by David Stone)

the Rideau Waterway for paddling. For information contact (613) 273-3255, www.rideauvalley.on.ca/cas/foleymnt.

Practical Information

Frontenac Provincial Park

- Park Season: open year-round.
- Park Permit: required for all park users, available from the Trail Centre at the park entrance during office hours.
- Camping: Frontenac has 48 backcountry campsites, grouped into clusters of 2–4 tent sites, each with its own tent pad and firepit and access to a shared privy. These should be booked in advance through the Ontario Parks Reservation Service, as they are popular, especially on weekends and holidays. Camping is restricted to two consecutive nights at any campsite cluster to ensure frequent turnover and so that

visitors may move easily through different areas of the park. Sites 1, 2 and 4 are along the excursion loop, and sites 3 and 5 are nearby.

- Information: park Trail Centre (613) 376-3489, Ontario Parks Reservation Service 1-888-668-7275, www.ontarioparks.com.

Maps & Publications

- The Friends of Frontenac Park have published an excellent 1:20,000 topographic map, complete with hiking trails, portages, campsites and many points of interest. It can be purchased at the Trail Centre and at many outdoor stores across the province. It is a must for hiking and paddling in the park.

Supplies, Accommodations & Attractions Outside the Park

- Frontenac Outfitters, on Bedford Road at the turnoff to the park, carries some basic supplies, and offers camping and canoe/kayak rentals. For information contact (613) 376-6220, www.frontenac-outfitters.com.
- More extensive supplies and accommodations are available in the nearby towns of Sydenham and Westport, or in the city of Kingston, half an hour's drive to the south.

Chapter 2

Bon Echo

Overview

Bon Echo Provincial Park is located in the Addington Highlands of eastern Ontario, midway between Napanee on Lake Ontario to the south and Pembroke on the Ottawa River to the north. The park's most prominent feature is Mazinaw Rock, a cliff that rises spectacularly out of Mazinaw Lake. Besides its geological interest, the cliff face also serves as the canvas for a collection of Native rock paintings and some carved lines of nineteenth century verse, so it is also of interest from the perspective of human history. The park straddles Mazinaw Lake, encompassing many kilometres of wild country on both sides, giving the outdoor enthusiast plenty of opportunities for hiking and paddling.

Bon Echo sits upon the Frontenac Axis, a finger of ancient bedrock that extends across southeastern Ontario toward the Adirondack Mountains. The rocks of Bon Echo formed between 1.5 and 1 billion years ago when magma solidified deep beneath the Earth's surface, forming a large mass of granite. Over the millennia that followed, tectonic forces compressed the granite and created a north-south fracture, pushing the eastern side up and the western side down. Glaciers scoured away the overlying sediment, and erosion by ice and water amplified the fracture, creating Mazinaw Lake — up to 145 metres deep — and Mazinaw Rock — over 100 metres high— an impressive total of 250 vertical metres.

Paddling along the base of the cliff, it is not difficult to see why Native people have long regarded the site as a place of great spiritual significance — a dramatic junction of earth, air and water, and a meeting place of the spirit and the human worlds. Some 260 red-ochre pictographs, the largest concentration discovered anywhere in Ontario, can be seen near the water-line at the base of Mazinaw Rock. They depict figures of importance to the Native people who painted them — creatures from the animal world, manitous from the spiritual world (including a splendid image of Mishepeshu, chief manitou of the underwater realm) and enigmatic images like the "picket fence" and numerous lines and squiggles whose meanings are unknown today. (For a more detailed discussion of the images see *Petroglyphs and Pictographs*, page 42.)

Clifftop view over the Mazinaw Narrows

Among these ancient pictographs are several lines of verse by nineteenth-century American poet Walt Whitman, a reminder of Bon Echo's more recent history. The Addington Highlands remained largely unexplored and undeveloped until the 1850s, when logging made its way into the area and the Addington Road was built between Kaladar and Denbigh. A few hardy settlers attempted to farm the land in the late 1800s, but the Shield terrain did not yield easily to agriculture and most farmers abandoned their efforts. Then at the end of the century a young dentist, Dr. Weston Price, brought his new bride to Mazinaw Lake for their honeymoon and was so impressed by the beauty of the place that in 1889 he purchased the parcel of land on both sides of the narrows. He built the Bon Echo Inn, which he named for the acoustical properties of the rock across the lake, and ran a thriving establishment for almost 20 years.

In 1910 he sold the inn to Flora MacDonald Denison, an exceptional woman of her time — owner of a successful Toronto dressmaking business, vigorous advocate of women's rights, and passionate devotee of the arts. Under her influence, and later that of her son (playwright Merrill Denison) and his wife (noted children's author Muriel Goggin Denison), the Bon Echo Inn became a cultural retreat. Distinguished members of the arts and letters community visited the resort, including six of the Group of Seven painters, portrait photographer Yousuf Karsh and such literary luminaries as

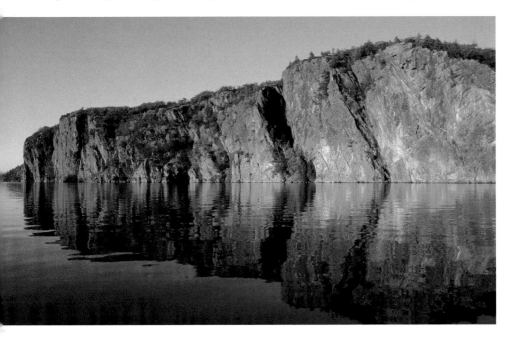

Mazinaw Rock

Morley Callaghan and Ernest Hemingway. Flora was a particular admirer of the works of Walt Whitman and she founded the Walt Whitman Club of Bon Echo. Before her death in 1921 she commissioned a memorial — several lines of verse from one of Whitman's poems — to be carved into Mazinaw Rock.

The Denison years at Bon Echo came to an end in 1936 when fire destroyed the inn. In 1959 Merrill Denison donated his 4.8 km² of property along the Mazinaw narrows to the provincial government. Bon Echo Park was established in 1965 and land was added in subsequent years, so that the park now covers 66 km². Meanwhile Hwy 41 replaced the muddy Addington Road in 1935, opening the Addington Highlands to cottagers and tourists.

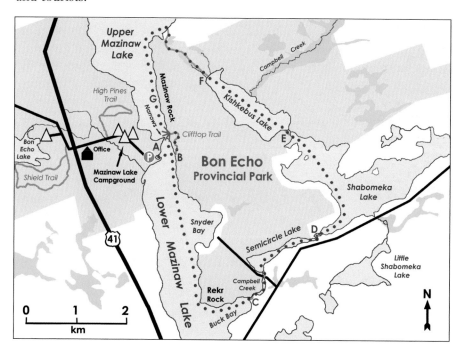

Access

- From the southwest, exit Hwy 401 at Belleville onto Hwy 37 north, continue 44 km to Hwy 7 and turn right, drive 22 km to Kaladar and turn left onto Hwy 41.
- From the southeast, exit Hwy 401 onto Hwy 41 at Napanee, and continue for 47 km to Kaladar.
- From Kaladar, drive north on Hwy 41 for 35 km to the Bon Echo park entrance on the right.
- Approaching from the north, take Hwy 41 south from the junction of

Hwy 41/28 at Denbigh, and drive 32 km to the Bon Echo park entrance on the left.

- Purchase a day-use or camping permit from the park office just inside the entrance.
- Continue straight past the office for 750 m. Turn right at the bottom of the hill, then almost immediately left, following the signs to the Mugwump Ferry, where there is a parking area and a dock from which to launch your kayak or canoe into the lagoon.

Mazinaw—Kishkebus Loop

This excursion combines a short hike to a superb clifftop lookout with a longish paddle around the Mazinaw–Kishkebus canoe route, including a stop at the fascinating pictographs on Mazinaw Rock. The paddling portion of the excursion is circular, so it can be done in either direction depending on the paddler's preferences and on wind conditions (which are more typically from the north than from the south and stronger in the afternoon than in the morning). Doing it in a clockwise direction gets the long (1500 m) portage over with near the start of the excursion, but it can mean a strenuous paddle up Mazinaw Lake into the wind at the end of the day. Doing the route counter-clockwise, as it is described here, reduces the risk of troublesome wind and it tackles the long portage after lunch when, presumably, most of the day's provisions will have been consumed, making the load a bit lighter on the shoulders.

- Main Route: 1.5 km hike, 15 km paddle, 1600 m portage(s)
- Alternative(s): 1.5 km hike, 25 km paddle, 200 m portage(s)

Route Description
1st Segment: Clifftop Trail (0.2 km paddle, 1.5 km hike)
From the launch **A** in the lagoon, paddle directly across Mazinaw Lake and leave your boat tied or pulled up on the dock on the opposite shore **B**. Follow the well-marked Clifftop Trail up the hill. A trail guide is available (from the park office or the Greystones Giftshop), which describes some of the cliff's natural features. The trail weaves through forested hollows and barren uplands, climbing more than 100 m — with the aid of a metal staircase up the steepest sections. It emerges atop Mazinaw Rock at the edge of the cliff, where three platforms offer glorious views over the lake and the forests beyond. Having taken in the scenery, return along the same trail to your boat.

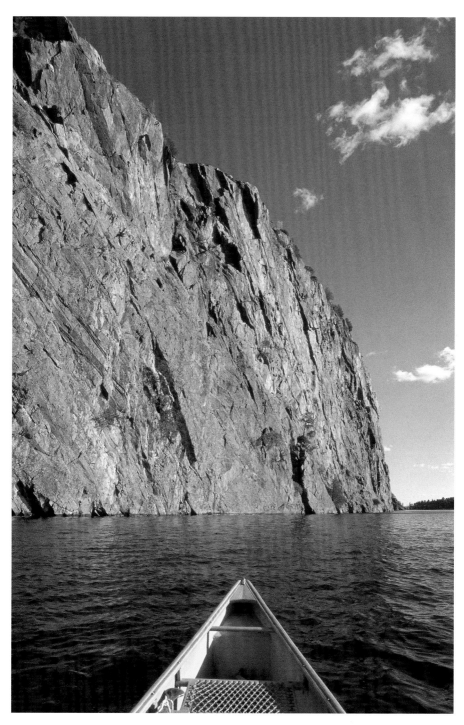

Approaching Mazinaw Rock

2nd Segment: Mazinaw Lake to Campbell Creek (4 km paddle)

From the dock **B** paddle south along the Mazinaw Lake shoreline, past Snyder Bay with its collection of cottages, and around the corner into Buck Bay where an imposing cliff, Rekr Rock, guards the entrance. The bay becomes shallow and sandy, narrowing toward the eastern end where Campbell Creek tumbles down a rocky channel into the lake **C**. This is the first portage of the day.

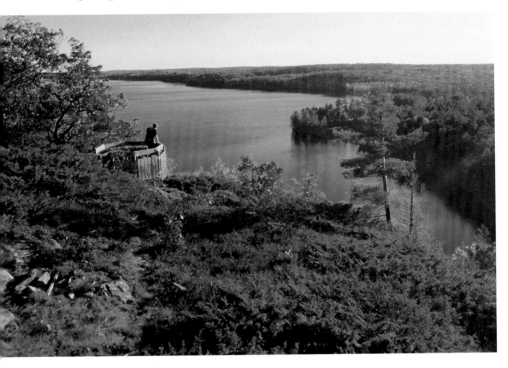

View from Clifftop Trail

3rd Segment: Campbell Creek to Kishkebus Lake (5.5 km paddle, 3–5 portages totalling 90–110 m)

This segment of the excursion follows Campbell Creek, wending its way upstream through Semicircle Lake and Shabomeka Lake into Kishkebus Lake. Depending on water levels and recent beaver activity, the route may have as many as five short portages, but it is often possible to lift, line or pole a boat across some of them. The first portage between Buck Bay and Campbell Creek is a short lift of only 5 m to the right of the channel to avoid a small jumble of rocks and logs. The next portage, just 0.5 km upstream, is 10 m to the right, this time to cross a gravel road leading to the cottages on Snyder Bay. On the other side of the portage is Semicircle

Lake, which is shallow and weedy for much of its 1.5 km length. At the eastern end D is a beaver dam lift-over followed a few metres later by a 20–30 m portage (either right or left) to bypass another dam, this one built by humans. Above the dam, Shabomeka Lake gives a welcome break from lifting and lugging, with several kilometres of paddling, first east and then north to the final short portage E — 60 m to the left — to skirt a rocky section of Campbell Creek between Shabomeka and Kishkebus lakes.

4th Segment: Kishkebus Lake to Mazinaw Lake (2 km paddle, 1500 m portage)

Kishkebus Lake, which is entirely within the boundary of Bon Echo Park, has no cottages or motorboat traffic to intrude on its peaceful atmosphere. There are several rocky knolls on the lake's east side that make pleasant places for a picnic lunch and a rest in preparation for the final leg of the excursion. At the north end of Kishkebus Lake, a small sandy beach F marks the start of the portage to Mazinaw Lake. The portage itself, though long, is not difficult. The well-tramped trail is easy to follow, with board-walks over boggy sections. The topography is fairly gentle, with a gradual rise for the first two-thirds of the distance, and a steeper descent for the last third, ending at a tiny gravelly put-in.

5th Segment: Homeward (3 km paddle)

From the portage, turn left and follow the shoreline of Mazinaw Lake, which heads west for 500 m and then rounds a point, turning south. Mazinaw Rock lies ahead, its magnificent cliffs towering dizzyingly above the lake. Paddle close to the base of the cliff G for a close-up view. Bands of multicoloured rock curve skyward. Ancient twisted cedar trees, hardy pines, oaks and colourful lichens cling precariously to the cliff face. And on flat sections of rock just above the waterline are Bon Echo's famous pictographs. Closer to the narrows the paintings are disappointingly faded, but here at the north end of the cliff, further removed from the wake of motorboats and the thoughtless handling of tourists, there are several wonderfully clear images. Continue along the cliff toward the narrows, past the lines of Walt Whitman verse, then cross over to the lagoon to end the excursion back at the launch A.

Alternative: Omit the Long Portage (1.5 km hike, 25 km paddle, 200 m portage)

Anyone allergic to long portages can omit the 1500 m portage between Kishkebus and Mazinaw lakes by turning the excursion into a linear route and paddling back down Campbell Creek from Kishkebus Lake. Without the portage the route is a strenuous 25 km with 6–10 short portages totalling about 200 m, and it requires a side-trip to the north of the Mazinaw Lake narrows to see the pictographs, so at the end of the day it will not feel any less demanding than the full circle route, long portage and all!

Other Paddling & Hiking Opportunities

Bon Echo Park has several excellent hiking trails. Two short ones, the High Pines Trail (1.6 km) and the Bon Echo Creek Trail (1.0 km), can be accessed from the Mazinaw Lake Campground. Along the Joeperry Road, which exits left at the park office and heads west, passing under Hwy 41, the Shield Trail (4.6 km) makes a pleasant half-day loop hike. Farther down the Joeperry Road is the trailhead for the longer, more demanding Abes & Essens Trail, which has three loops — 4 km around Clutes Lake, or 9 km around both Clutes Lake and Essens Lake, or 17 km, which also takes in Little Rock and Abes lakes to the north. It is possible to do the entire loop in a single, strenuous day, or you can break it into a two-day backpacking trip, camping overnight in one of the interior sites along the trail.

For paddling on a smaller scale, Joeperry, Pearson and Bon Echo lakes, accessed from the Joeperry Road, are peaceful lakes, free of motorboat traffic, that give short paddling opportunities within the park. The shorelines of Joeperry and Pearson lakes are dotted with interior, paddle-in campsites, while Bon Echo Lake is the site of the park's group campground area.

On a larger scale, Mazinaw Lake is part of the Mississippi River system, stretching some 225 km from the Madawaska Highlands north of Bon Echo to the Ottawa River in the east. Along this river there are opportunities for multi-day paddling excursions that demand whitewater skills and stamina for lengthy portages.

Practical Information

Bon Echo Provincial Park
- Park Season: open late April to late October.
- Park Permit: required for all Bon Echo Park users, available from the office at the park entrance.
- Camping: Bon Echo has a large, well-serviced campground with 526 sites, 133 of which are electrical. The campsites are organized into two main areas — the Mazinaw Lake Campground to the east of Hwy 41 and the Hardwood Hill Campground to the west. These sites are popular,

and should be reserved in advance during the summer months. Bon Echo also has 30 interior camp sites for backpackers and paddlers, located along the Abes & Essens hiking trail and on the shores of Joeperry and Pearson lakes.

Mysterious "picket fence" pictograph

- Information: park office (613) 336-2228, Ontario Parks Reservation Service 1-888-668-7275, www.ontarioparks.com.
- Friends of Bon Echo Park is a non-profit association that assists Bon Echo Park staff in providing educational programs and publications. They operate the park's ferry and tour boats, and run the Greystones Giftshop. Contact the Friends at (613) 336-9863, www.mazinaw.on.ca/fobecho.

Maps & Publications
- Chrismar Mapping Services has published, as part of their Adventure Map series, an excellent, waterproof, 1:30,000 topographic map of Bon Echo Park and the surrounding area, showing the lakes, rivers and portages, and the park's hiking trails and interior campsites. The reverse side of the map gives descriptions of the natural features and human history of the park. This map is a must for travelling in the park, and can be purchased at outdoor stores across the province.
- The Friends of Bon Echo Park have published guides for several of the park's trails, obtainable from the park office and the Greystones Giftshop.

Supplies & Accommodations Outside the Park
- Basic supplies are available in the nearby towns of Cloyne and Kaladar, 5 km and 35 km to the south of the park respectively, or in Denbigh, 32 km to the north.
- The nearest larger towns for more extensive supplies are Tweed, 60 km to the southwest of the park on Hwy 37, and Napanee, 82 km to the south at the junction of Hwys 41 and 401.
- Addington Highlands tourism information is available at the County of Lennox & Addington, (613) 354-4883, www.lennox-addington.on.ca.

Petroglyphs and Pictographs

On scattered rock faces across the Canadian Shield the observant traveller will find some remarkable images. Some are carved; others are painted. They are the picture-writings of the Shield's Native peoples, and they tell tales of ancient journeys, both secular and spiritual.

Petroglyphs are carved images, chiselled with primitive tools into the rock. They occur only rarely in Ontario, and the best-known examples are those at Petroglyphs Provincial Park near Peterborough (see Chapter 5).

Horse and spheres at Agawa Rock, Lake Superior

Pictographs are paintings, typically done in vibrant red-ochre — a pigment made from iron oxide mined from veins in the bedrock, ground into powder and mixed with animal fat or fish oil to form a paste. Fine examples of pictographs can be seen on Mazinaw Rock in Bon Echo Provincial Park (Chapter 2) and Agawa Rock on Lake Superior (Chapter 12), but they are not uncommon along paddling routes all across Ontario's Shield.

The precise age of the images is impossible to determine, as reliable scientific methods do not exist for dating petroglyphs and pictographs. Only by "relative" dating — comparing the paintings and carvings with associated artifacts whose age can be precisely carbon-dated — is it possible to estimate their place in history. It seems that the practice practice of picture-writing may have originated across the Canadian Shield during the era of the Woodland

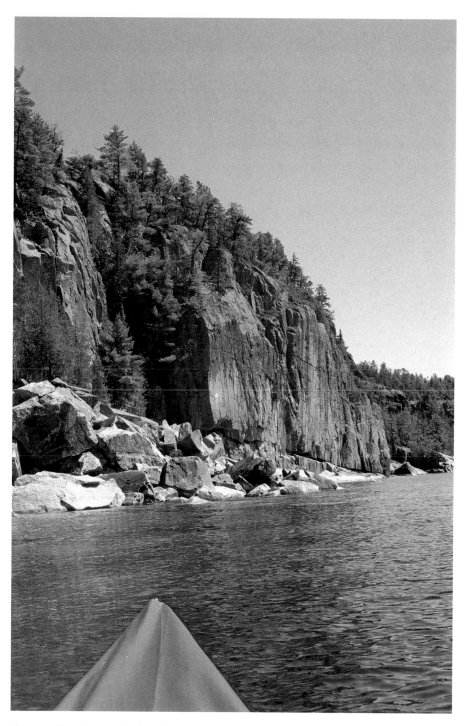

Approach to Agawa Rock, Lake Superior

Mishepeshu and canoe on Agawa Rock

People between 1000 and 2000 years ago, but certainly by 600–800 years ago it was practised among the Algonkian-speaking tribes — the Ojibwe of Lake Superior and northeastern Ontario, the Cree of northwestern Ontario, and the Odawa of the Bruce Peninsula and Manitoulin Island. It continued during the early years of contact with Europeans but came to an end at the beginning of the twentieth century when modern North American life irrevocably altered the ancient Native culture.

Some of the images seem to be secular in character, relaying messages to other travellers along the same route or commemorating special events. More common, however, are sacred images, which depict Native manitous and illustrate spiritual teachings.

Manitous are the gods of the Native world. Like gods of Western religions, manitous are spiritual beings with great powers, some good, some evil. But unlike many Western gods, Native manitous inhabit the same physical world as people, and are present in the earth, water, air, and in the animals living there. The "good" manitous are those in the upper realm of the natural world—the Thunderbirds and the Four Winds of the air, and terrestrial manitous like Bear and Wolf. The "evil" manitous are those in the subterranean world — Snake, who lives in holes in the earth, and the fascinating horned lynx, Mishepeshu, who inhabits the underwater kingdom and controls the wind and waves with a flick of his powerful tail. Above them all are Gitche Manitou, the supreme spirit, creator and overseer of all things, and his messenger on earth, Nanabosho, a delightfully impetuous manitou who serves as protector for the Native peoples.

In the harsh environment of the Canadian Shield, Natives who are able to communicate with the manitous can access the manitous' powers and thus gain the advantage in hunting, in battle and in healing. Sites where the natural elements of earth, water and air meet — where a cliff-face plunges into a deep lake, for instance, are considered spiritual sites. There, the realms of humans and manitous converge, and it is therefore at these sites that picture-writings are most commonly found.

At first glance, many of the images may seem disappointing. They have become faded and worn from centuries of erosion by wind and water, and in recent times by corrosion from air pollution and defacement by modern travellers. Interpretation of the images can be perplexing, as there are no written records to accompany them, so the lines and squiggles and faint red washes are difficult to appreciate. There are a number of excellent guidebooks, however, which help to shed some light on the images and place them in the context of the Native culture that created them (see, for instance, *Reading Rock Art* by Grace Rajnovich, published by Natural Heritage/Natural History Inc., 1994). And occasionally one comes across an image that is crisp and vibrant — like the Mishepeshu figures at Bon Echo and Agawa Rock — whose impact is positively electrifying!

Pictograph on Mazinaw Rock

Mishepeshu on Mazinaw Rock

Chapter 3

Achray

Overview

The familiar picture-postcard image of Algonquin Park is a landscape of rolling hills dotted with sparkling lakes and blanketed with colourful maples. This is the Algonquin of the popular "Highway 60 corridor," a highland area on the park's southwestern side that is easily accessible from the population centres of southern Ontario. Algonquin Park is an enormous place, however, with a total area of 7,650 km^2 stretching far to the north and east and encompassing a great variety of landscapes. Achray, for instance, tucked away on Algonquin's eastern side, has a character that is surprisingly and pleasantly different.

The variation between west and east is closely tied to the difference in elevation between them. The western highlands are generally loftier, many of the hills rising at least 200 metres higher than the terrain on the eastern side of the park. Moisture-laden air carried by the prevailing winds off Georgian Bay cools as it rises up the western slopes and sheds its moisture over the highlands in the form of rain or snow. The air that then descends to the eastern lowlands is dry—an average of 10% drier—causing a "rainshadow" effect in the lee of the highland hills.

As the last glacier retreated northward some 10,000 years ago the lowlands in the east provided a natural conduit for glacial meltwater. For several centuries a massive river ran through the Achray area, draining glacial Lake Algonquin to the northwest, sweeping through present-day Grand and Stratton lakes and surging down the Barron Canyon on its way to the Champlain Sea in the southeast. It carried away with it all the area's fine-grained silts and soils, and left behind a coarse mixture of sand and rock.

The resulting terrain in the east is therefore generally drier and less fertile than the land in the west and is unable to support the variety of vegetation that thrives in the relatively moist, rich environment of the highlands. For vegetation that can tolerate dry conditions, however, it is a superb home. Pines — white, red and jack — are found in abundance here, and the park's eastern side has been a plentiful source of pine timber for more than a century. Red oaks thrive here too, and blueberry bushes

High Falls cascade

flourish on the sunny hillsides — the berries and acorns nourishing the sizeable population of black bears living in this area of the park.

For the outdoor enthusiast Achray provides splendid opportunities for paddling and hiking, with routes that are more remote and typically less congested than those of Algonquin's western side. Achray's most celebrated natural feature, the Barron Canyon, can be approached on foot by means of a short interpretive trail or by canoe or kayak from one of several access points along the Barron River. The loops of the Berm Lake and Eastern Pines Backpacking Trails encompass 15 km of rugged hiking, and Achray's lakes afford many kilometres of paddling and access to the extensive network of Algonquin's other paddling routes.

Access

- From Hwy 17 between Pembroke and Petawawa exit west onto Hwy 28, then turn immediately right onto the Barron Canyon Road.
- Follow the Barron Canyon Road for 26 km to the Sand Lake Gate at the entrance to the park, and purchase a permit from the park office.
- Continue along the Barron Canyon Road to the access point indicated at the start of each excursion below.

Barron Canyon

This excursion spends a day exploring the Barron Canyon, combining the bird's eye perspective of the clifftop hiking trail with the intimate view from the Barron River below, for a comprehensive look at the canyon's geology and natural history. An interpretive booklet with sections corresponding to numbered posts on the trail gives detailed information about the features found along the way. It is available for a nominal fee at the Barron Canyon trailhead or the Sand Lake Gate.

• **Main Route: 1.5 km hike, 8–16 km paddle, 1180 m portage(s)**

Barron Canyon cliffs from the Barron River

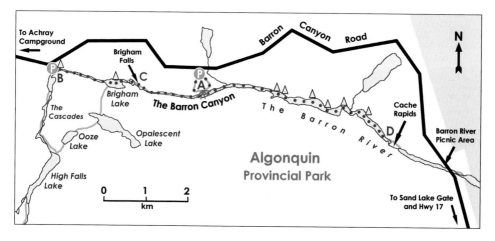

Access

- From the Sand Lake Gate continue for 10 km along the Barron Canyon Road and exit into the Barron Canyon Trail parking lot on the left.

Route Description

1st Segment: Barron Canyon Interpretive Trail (1.5 km hike)

The trail **A** winds quickly upward from the parking lot to the cliff over-looking the Barron Canyon, then makes its way through the pine trees along the rim of the cliff for 0.5 km before looping back down the hill.

The canyon was formed along a geological fault—a line of weakness in the ancient bedrock—that became gradually enlarged by erosion. Chunks of the rock walls on either side were pried loose by frost, widening the fault and accumulating rocky debris called "talus" at the base of the cliffs. Water flowing between the walls also helped to broaden the fault. Peering over the edge today, it may be difficult to imagine that the placid river 100 m below was once a thundering torrent. Ten thousand years ago glacial meltwater from Lake Algonquin, predecessor to the Great Lakes, drained through the canyon on its way eastward to the Atlantic, its capacity estimated to have far exceeded that of the modern-day St. Lawrence River. Then, as the glacier retreated, other outlets were uncovered further north and the Barron River diminished to a relative trickle. The canyon became home to an unusual collection of creatures—crustaceans, fish and plants—relics from the Ice Age more commonly found today in the arctic than in the temperate climate of the south.

2nd Segment: Drive to Brigham Lake

Back at the parking lot, drive 4 km further along the Barron Canyon Road to the Brigham Lake access, which exits on the left. Leave your vehicle in the parking area and carry your boat down the steep path to the Barron River below.

3rd Segment: Barron Canyon from Below (4–8 km paddle, 540 m portage)

From the launch **B** paddle downstream along the Barron River for 1.5 km to Brigham Lake. At the eastern end of the lake two portages, 100 m and 440 m, bypass rough sections of rapids and falls.

At the top of the waterfall along the second portage, an iron ring can be seen in one of the rocks beside the path **C**, a remnant of the river's log-drive days. For a century, from the 1830s to the 1930s, the Barron River was a major transport route for timber. Trees felled in Algonquin's interior during the winter were sent down river during the spring runoff to mills along the Ottawa River, and from there by boat to markets in Europe and America. Booms were constructed to marshall logs on the lakes along the river, and a system of dams and chutes was used to flush the timber over rapids and falls. Brigham Lake was such a marshalling place, and Brigham Falls the location of a dam and chute.

Beyond the falls the river becomes placid again and the walls rise steeply on both sides. The Barron Canyon is a stunning spectacle from below, its cliffs towering dizzyingly overhead, and the enormous piles of talus at its

Barron Canyon Trail lookout (photo by David Stone)

base a sobering reminder of the fragility of those cliffs. On the rocks high above the river, one can make out miniature hikers enjoying the views from the Barron Canyon Trail. The cliff gradually dwindles beyond the trail, but the river continues gently on its way for several kilometres to the Cache Rapids **D**, site of another logging chute. Paddle as far along the river as time and energy allow before turning back.

4th Segment: Homeward (4–8 km paddle, 540 m portage)

Return upstream via the outward route through the canyon, over the portages and through Brigham Lake to the launch.

Berm Lake and High Falls

This excursion begins with a hike around the pretty Berm Lake Trail, then takes to the water for a paddle through Grand and Stratton lakes to High Falls where the Barron River tumbles 29 m over a series of beautiful rocky ledges. Upon returning to Grand Lake, you may opt for an extension of the excursion to visit the cliffs and pictographs of Carcajou Bay.

• Main Route: 4.5 km hike, 16–21 km paddle, 60 m portage(s)

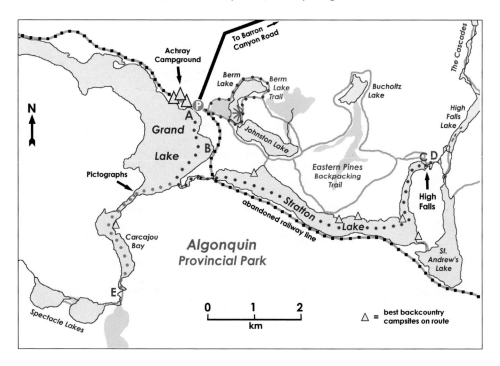

51

Access

- From the Sand Lake Gate continue for 19 km along the Barron Canyon Road, then turn left and follow the Achray campground access road for 5 km. Leave your car in one of the parking areas at the end of the road, adjacent to the abandoned railway line.

Route Description

1st Segment: Berm Lake Trail (4.5 km hike)

The Berm Lake Trail begins at the east side of the parking lot. Pick up an interpretive booklet from the box at the trailhead (or in advance from the Sand Lake Gate). The booklet, which has sections corresponding to numbered posts along the trail, discusses the ecology of the Achray area and introduces some of its characteristic features.

The trail winds from the trailhead through woodland for 0.7 km to the edge of Berm Lake, then circles the lake in a clockwise direction. At first the trail hugs the shoreline, but at the eastern end of the lake it turns slightly inland and climbs to a ridge overlooking the lake and the marshland at its western end. The trail then descends along a narrow finger of land between Berm Lake and Johnston Lake, where there are pleasant views in both directions, before making its way back to the parking lot.

Exchange the hiking boots for a paddle and a PFD, and launch your boat from the beach at Grand Lake.

2nd Segment: Grand Lake to High Falls (8 km paddle, 30 m portage)

From the launch A paddle along the left-hand shoreline of Grand Lake. During the summer of 1916 this shore was frequented by Tom Thomson. Although the artist worked at Achray as a fire ranger, the work in this region for which he is most remembered is his collection of sketches and oil paintings inspired by the landscape. Most famous among them is *The Jack Pine*, a scene looking south across Grand Lake toward Carcajou Bay from a site B about 1 km along the shore from the launch. The cabin at Achray where Thomson lived has been restored as a mini-museum that is open to the public during the summer.

Continue along the shoreline to a sandy spit at the lake's southeastern corner, then curve sharply to the left into the Barron River. Follow the river downstream, taking a short portage around a dam and passing under an abandoned railway bridge. Beyond the bridge Stratton Lake stretches 4 km to the east, then turns abruptly north for another 1.5 km, at which point it narrows and cascades over High Falls into the Barron River. Paddle the full length of the lake and pull your boat ashore on the rocks to the left-hand side at the narrows C.

View from High Falls lookout

3rd Segment: High Falls (0.5 km hike)

High Falls begins as a series of smooth waterslides and pretty pools with rock outcrops sloping gracefully into the water, but it finishes with the river plunging over a precipice **D** — accompanied during the spring runoff by a great deal of sound and fury. A maze of trails crisscrosses the rocks between the takeout at the top and the waterfall at the bottom, and there are many places for a scenic picnic lunch — and even a refreshing dip in one of the pools — before you begin the homeward journey.

4th Segment: Homeward (8–13 km paddle, 30 m portage)

Return via the outward route through Stratton Lake and up the river into Grand Lake. If you have the time and energy, turn left at the top of the river and paddle into Carcajou Bay. This narrow arm of the lake has some lovely rock walls along its shores, and a pretty waterfall at its south end where Carcajou Creek tumbles through a cleft in the rocks **E**. On the west side of the entrance to Carcajou Bay several pictographs are visible on the cliffs at the waterline — images painted by Native travellers centuries ago as a spiritual or historical record, badly faded now after years of erosion by waves and ice, and handling by subsequent paddlers. From the pictographs, paddle north across the lake to the launch **A** to finish the day's excursion.

Other Paddling & Hiking Opportunities

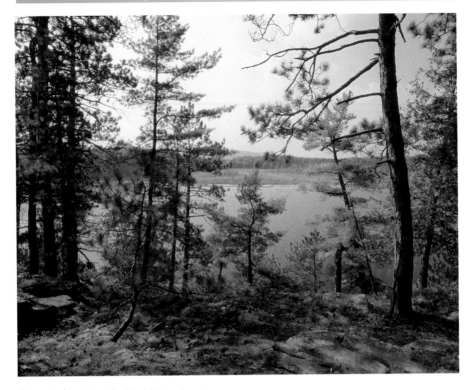

Berm Lake (photo by David Stone)

Paddling

- There are many opportunities for paddling day-trips at Achray. From Grand Lake it is possible to visit the Spectacle Lakes to the south (12 km paddle with 400 m of portages), or to poke along the shoreline of Grand Lake itself, which stretches west from the campground for 10 km. Sec Lake, at the east end of the park, also offers a pleasant paddle (accessible from the Barron Canyon road 3 km to the east of the Sand Lake Gate).
- The Barron River can be undertaken as a multi-day excursion, beginning at Grand Lake and paddling downstream through Stratton, St. Andrews and High Falls lakes and down the Barron Canyon to the Barron River picnic area (23 km paddle with 10 portages totalling 2960 m). Except for a brief period of heavy flow during the spring melt, the river can also be paddled in the upstream direction. A possible variation for the return trip is to paddle through Opalescent and Ooze lakes, adding 320 m of portage length but avoiding the potentially faster water of the Cascades.

Hiking

- The Eastern Pines Backpacking Trail has loops of 6 and 15 km beginning at the Achray campground parking lot and extending east to High Falls, taking in Johnston, Bucholtz and Stratton lakes en route. For people not wishing to backpack the entire trail, the Johnston Lake loop can be combined with the Berm Lake trail into a day-hike from the Achray campground; or the Bucholtz Lake loop can be done as a day-hike from one of the paddle-in campsites on Stratton Lake.

Practical Information

Algonquin Provincial Park, Achray

- Park Season: open late April to mid-October.
- Park Permit: required for all Achray users, available from the Sand Lake Gate office at the park entrance.
- Camping: The Achray campground has 39 sites and basic toilet facilities but no showers or laundry. Sites need to be reserved in advance for the busy summer months. There are also dozens of interior sites scattered around the lakes and along the Eastern Pines Backpacking Trail. Achray also has a yurt (a permanent, tent-like structure containing basic furnishings) available for rent.
- Information: Algonquin–Achray general information (705) 633-5572, Sand Lake Gate (613) 732-555, Ontario Parks Reservation Service 1-888-668-7275, www.ontarioparks.com.

Maps & Publications

- *Canoe Routes of Algonquin Provincial Park* and *Backpacking Trails of Algonquin Provincial Park*, maps published by the Friends of Algonquin Park, contain detailed information on the park's paddling and hiking routes, including portages, campsites and other points of interest. The maps are available from the Sand Lake Gate office and from many out door stores across the province.
- Chrismar Mapping Services has published, as part of their Adventure Map series, an excellent, waterproof 1:40,000 Barron/Achray topographic map. On the map side it shows the hiking trails, portages, campsites and other features, and on the reverse side it gives a brief natural history and practical information about this area of Algonquin Park. It is widely available from outdoor stores.
- Hiking trail guides for the Barron Canyon Trail and the Berm Lake Trail are available from boxes at the trailheads and from the Sand Lake Gate office. Numbered posts along the trails correspond to sections in

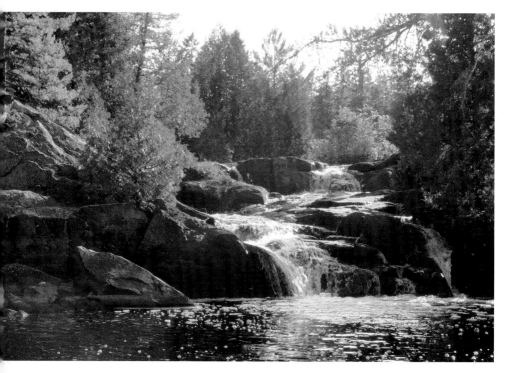

Carcajou Falls (photo by David Stone)

the trail guides that discuss the natural and human historical background of features seen along the way.

- The Friends of Algonquin Park have produced an excellent series of interpretive booklets about the flora and fauna of the park. They are available at the Sand Lake Gate office.

Supplies & Accommodations Outside the Park

- Supplies and accommodations are not readily available for visitors to Achray, so be sure to stock up in advance. The closest town is Pembroke, 50 km to the east of the Achray campground at the start of the Barron Canyon Road.
- Algonquin Portage Outfitters, located 6 km from the start of the Barron Canyon Road, has basic groceries, camping supplies and souvenirs, and also offers accommodations and rentals of canoes and camping supplies. For information contact (613) 735-1795, www.algonquinportage.com.

Pine Trees of Ontario's Shield

Ontario's shield is home to three types of pine trees — white, red and jack. Belonging to the same taxonomic family of plants, they have many common characteristics — those that make them pine trees. They are all cone-bearing (coniferous), they keep their foliage year-round (evergreen) and their foliage takes the form of long needles.

Beyond these distinguishing features, the three pines also share similar habitats. They are found in the relatively cool, moist climate of temperate North America. The white pine grows across much of Ontario's shield, from the Frontenac Axis in the far southeast to the edge of the boreal forest along Lake Superior in the northwest. The red pine is restricted to the southerly part of this zone. The jack pine thrives in the northerly part, and is found in abundance in boreal habitats. In fact it ranges so far north that it has been designated the official tree of the Northwest Territories. The white pine is Ontario's provincial tree.

Within this broad geographic range, the three pines all prefer similar micro-environments. They thrive in well-drained, slightly acidic, mineral-rich, sandy soil (though the jack pine seems to be able grow where there is almost no soil at all —sometimes in the tiniest crevice on an apparently bare rock face!). They are also sun-loving, typically making

White pines at Silent Lake

their home on rocky shorelines and promontories, or at the tops of cliffs where they receive maximum exposure to light.

They reproduce well in areas where forest fire has cleared away the competing vegetation (including the parent trees) and burned off the surface litter, leaving an exposed mineral bed in which the seedlings may grow. The jack pine, being the least shade-tolerant of the three pines and the fastest to germinate and sprout, has carried this reliance on fire to an adaptive extreme. While the white and red pines release seeds annually, leaving reproduction largely to chance, jack pine cones remain closed for up to 25 years until a fire melts the resinous seal, allowing the seeds to scatter into an environment that is ideal for growth.

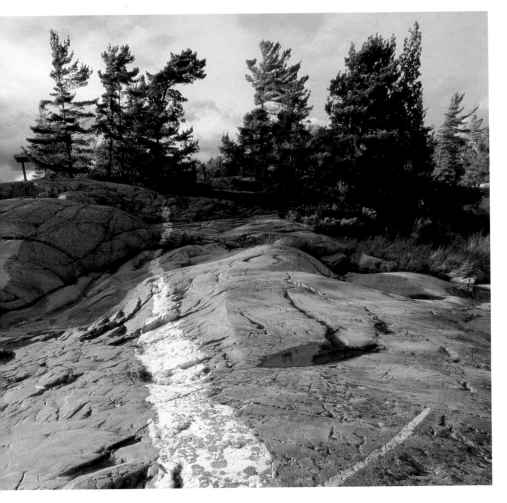

White pines on Georgian Bay coast, Killarney

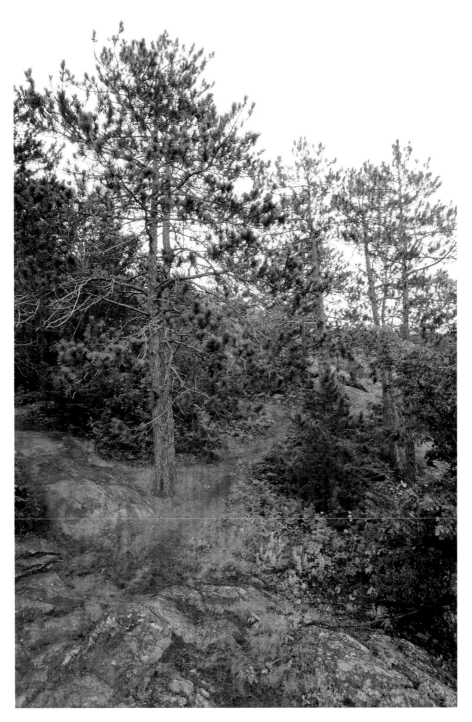

Red pines at Eagle's Nest, Bancroft

	White Pine	Red Pine	Jack Pine
General Appearance	windblown tops asymmetrical branches feathery foliage	straight symmetrical branches coarse, spiky foliage	straggly, sprawling asymmetrical drooping branches
Height	25–35 m typical 45 m possible	20–25 m typical 40–45 m possible	5–20 m typical 30 m possible
Needles	bundles of 5 needles 5–10 cm long slender, straight, fluffy light blue-green	bundles of 2 needles 10–15 cm long coarse, straight dark green	bundles of 2 needles 2–5 cm long coarse, twisted dark green
Bark	young: smooth, grey mature: grey-brown, furrowed	reddish-brown deeply furrowed or scaly/flaky	dark brown-grey rough/flaky
Cones	slender, tapered 8–20 cm long dark scales when open	short, rounded 5–8 cm long reddish scales when open	slender, curved 3–8 cm long typically tightly closed
Seeds	light crop annually large crop every 3–5 years dispersal: wind, animals	light crop annually large crop every 3-7 years dispersal: wind, animals	crop released by heat of fire and dispersed by wind and gravity
Roots	several major roots: widespread and moderately deep	tap-root: deep (to 4.5 m) lateral roots: widespread and moderately deep	tap-root: deep (to 3 m) lateral roots: shallow and sprawling
Age	commonly 200 years maximum 400–500 years	commonly 150-200 years maximum 400 years	commonly 75 years maximum 200–250 years
Human Uses	historical: ship masts modern: carpentry, furniture, wood trims and panels, Christmas trees	structural timber poles, railroad ties	pulp and paper poles, railroad ties

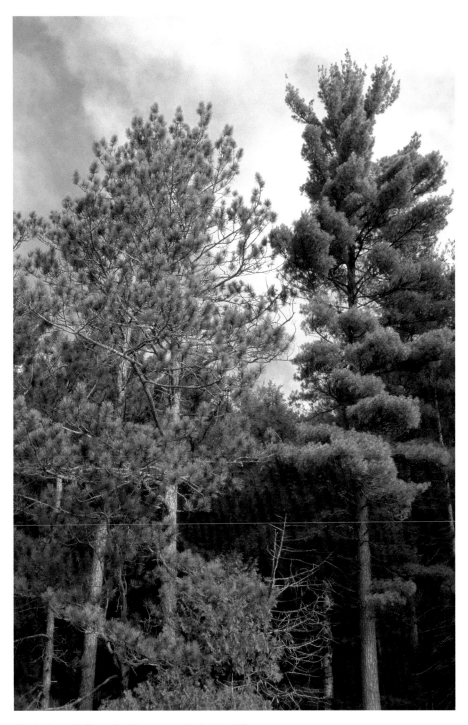

Red pines (left) and white pines (right) in Killarney

Chapter 4

Silent Lake

Overview

Silent Lake Provincial Park is located 23 km south of Bancroft where the highlands of Haliburton, Hastings and the Kawarthas converge. Silent Lake is a small park compared with some of its better-known neighbours — only 14 km² compared with Bon Echo's 66 km² or Algonquin's massive 7,653 km². It lacks the dramatic physical features of those parks, not having a Mazinaw Rock, a High Falls or a Centennial Ridge. But Silent Lake has a subtle, peaceful charm of its own, with small rocky islands, meandering creeks, and beaver-dammed marshlands. And while the park may not provide weeks of backcountry adventure, it does afford a weekend's enjoyable hiking and paddling within easy reach of the population centres of southern Ontario.

The Bancroft region is famous for its minerals. Bancroft sits atop the Grenville Province of the Canadian Shield, formed between 1.5 and 1 billion years ago when a group of small continents collided with each other and then rammed into the older Southern Province to the northwest. The original rocks that belonged to each of the small continents, and the ocean sediments and volcanic material caught between them, were compressed together and uplifted during the

Sunset across Silent Lake

collision. The result was the lofty Grenville mountain range, composed of complex mineral-rich metamorphic rocks. Glaciers subsequently eroded the range into the gentle rounded hills that make up the landscape today, and exposed the minerals once buried at the roots of the mountains. These minerals were discovered by prospectors in the late 1800s, and mining became an important part of Bancroft's economy in the early decades of the 1900s, with several hundred small mines springing into

Silent Lake boat launch

operation. Gemstones such as sodalite, garnet and corundum were quarried, as were more mundane minerals — feldspar and nepheline (used in the ceramic industry), mica (once used for electrical insulating), talc (also used for insulation, and for ointments and powders in the cosmetic industry), graphite (used, among other things, in the manufacture of pencils), marble and granite (for building construction) and uranium (for the nuclear industry). Bancroft's mines are still busy places, but today it is tourists, rather than miners, who rummage through the rubble.

Mining was not the only human endeavour in the area. Silent Lake was logged extensively during the mid-1800s. Later in the century the Patterson family homesteaded at the head of the lake and attempted, no doubt with considerable frustration, to farm the unyielding land. In 1927 Alfred Greene, an American newspaperman, bought the property and built an exclusive hunting and fishing lodge at the lake, attracting wealthy visitors hungry for venison and lake trout. Six Point Lodge operated successfully under the Greene family for 40 years. The land was repurchased by the Crown in 1967, and Silent Lake Provincial Park was opened in 1975. As a natural environment park, Silent Lake encourages low-impact activities like hiking, paddling and catch-and-release fishing, and it prohibits motorboats from its lakes and motorized vehicles from its trails — making the landscape pleasantly silent once again.

Paddling through Silent Lake marshland

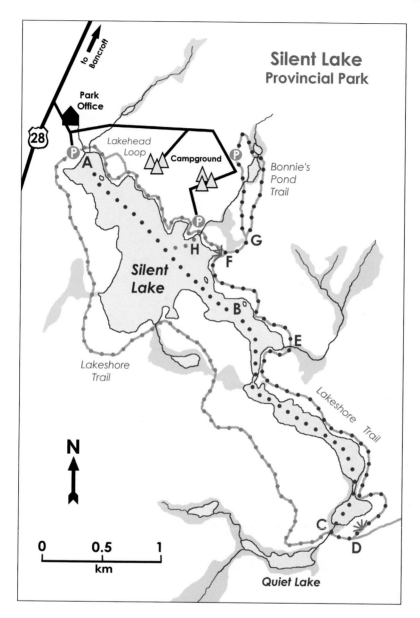

Access

- Take Hwy 28 north 75 km from Peterborough and exit to the right into Silent Lake Provincial Park, or south 23 km from Bancroft and exit left into the park.
- Purchase a permit from the park office just inside the entrance.
- Immediately past the office turn right to the day-use area where there is ample parking and a beach with a dock from which to launch your boat.

Silent Lake and Bonnie's Pond

The small size of Silent Lake Park rather limits the extent and variety of its opportunities for paddling and hiking. Silent Lake is only 4 km long. As it is not part of any larger navigable water system, it can be thoroughly explored in less than a day's paddle. On foot, the Bonnie's Pond Trail, at only 3.5 km, is an easy half-morning's stroll. The Lakeshore Trail is a longer hike of 15 km around the perimeter of the lake. The trail's route along the northeastern side of the lake hugs the shoreline quite closely, giving some lovely views; on the southwestern side the trail follows a less interesting inland route for much of the way. This excursion combines, in a roundabout way, the best of the park's features into a single day-long outing.

- Main Route: 11 km hike, 8 km paddle
- Alternative(s): 4–15 km hike, 8 km paddle

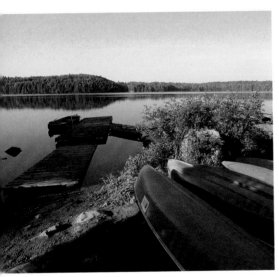

Silent Lake boat launch

Route Description

1st Segment: Silent Lake to the Boardwalk (4 km paddle)

From the launch **A** paddle southeast down the lake. The left-hand shoreline, adjacent to the campground and beaches, is usually bustling with red canoes from the park's rental fleet. The right-hand shore is somewhat quieter. Three small rocky islands are scattered along the route. The last of these **B**, 2 km down the left-hand shore, is particularly beautiful. A stone bench perched upon the rock bears a poignant memorial to a young woman, Alison Jayne Edwards (1972–2001), who loved to visit the park as a child and whose family erected the bench after her untimely death. Just past this island the lake jogs around a corner, first to the right, then to the left. A kilometre beyond the jog the lake narrows through a marshy area, then opens into a quiet bay. Cross the bay and follow a small creek for several metres upstream, where a boardwalk blocks the channel **C**. Tie your kayak or canoe to it, or pull your boat ashore, and proceed from there on foot.

Alison Jayne Edwards memorial bench

2nd Segment: Lakeshore Trail to Silent Lake Lookout (4 km hike)

Follow the boardwalk toward the left and continue along the track that climbs the hill to the south. Turn left 200 m up the hill **D** onto a narrower, rougher trail. Near the start of this trail is a pleasing lookout over the bay at the end of Silent Lake. Beyond the lookout the trail passes through an airy maple forest, then curves down a gully back to the shore. Crossing over a headland shaded by pine and hemlock trees, it emerges at another boardwalk over another marshy stream **E** with a lovely rocky outcrop in the middle. Several inland diversions and several rocky outcrops later, the trail climbs to the Silent Lake Lookout **F**, where a group of enthusiastic red pine trees has almost succeeded in obscuring the view.

3rd Segment: Bonnie's Pond Trail (3 km hike)

A few metres past the lookout, the Bonnie's Pond Trail exits inland, to the right. After skirting a marshy area, the trail forks **G**. Take the right-hand fork and continue up a gentle hill to the edge of Bonnie's Pond. The pond's name comes from the unfortunate workhorse who drowned there while hauling logs across the thinning spring ice.

Bonnie's Pond is more bog-like than pond-like now, its open water gradually filling in, illustrating the process of natural succession seen

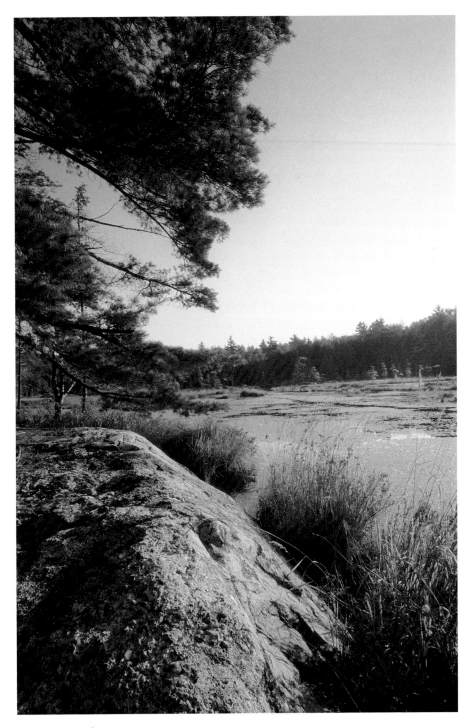

Bonnie's Pond

frequently across the Shield. Rotting vegetation in a shallow lake forms mats that are hospitable to marshland mosses and shrubs. As these plants die their litter accumulates and the mats thicken. Larger plants can then take root — tamaracks and alders first, then spruce and cedar, until eventually the land closes across the water.

Beyond the pond the trail climbs more steeply to a parking lot at the top of the hill, then returns toward Silent Lake, crossing a pretty stream and meandering through a hardwood forest.

4th Segment: Homeward (4 km hike, 4 km paddle)

Back at the Lakeshore Trail turn left and retrace the outward route to the boardwalk. Collect your boat, and paddle back up Silent Lake to the launch A. The incongruous strip of bright green grass at the day-use beach can be seen from far down the lake, serving as a beacon for the return trip.

Alternative 1: Shorten the Hike (4 km hike, 8 km paddle)

If you want to spend more of the day exploring the lake by boat and less time on land, the hike can be shortened by leaving out most of the Lakeshore Trail and hiking only the Bonnie's Pond Trail. Pull your boat ashore 1.2 km from the launch A at the park's canoe rental dock H. Follow the Lakeshore Trail for 0.5 km across the small stream south of the dock and up the hill to the Bonnie's Pond Trail and the Silent Lake Lookout F. This reduces the hike to only 4 km, and allows time to paddle the entire shoreline of the lake at a leisurely pace.

Alternative 2: Two Days of Excursions (4 + 15 km hike, 8 km paddle)

After spending one day doing the "Shorten the Hike" alternative, you may spend a second day hiking the entire 15 km of the Lakeshore Trail, starting at one of the access points between the day-use area A and the canoe rental dock H.

Other Paddling & Hiking Opportunities

Paddling

- Many lakes in the Bancroft area can be explored by boat. The largest of these are Eels Lake and Paudash Lake located on the west side of Hwy 28. Eels Lake is a short distance south and Paudash Lake a short distance north of the Silent Lake Provincial Park entrance. Both lakes are lined with cottages and can be busy with motorboat traffic.

Hiking

- The Lakehead Loop is a very short trail (1.5 km) that starts from Silent Lake day-use area and follows the shoreline briefly, then cuts over a wooded headland back to the parking lot.
- The Eagle's Nest Lookout, another very short trail, leads to a splendid view over the York River Valley. It is accessed from Hwy 62 on the north side of Bancroft, where a signpost points the way up a steep road to a parking area near the top of the hill.
- The Hastings Heritage Trail is a 156 km linear trail that runs from Glen Ross near Trenton to Lake St. Peter just north of Bancroft. It is the railbed of the former Central Ontario Railway, which has been converted to a multi-use trail that is shared by hikers, bicycles, ATVs and snowmobiles.

Other Attractions

- Silent Lake Provincial Park has 19 km of multi-use trails, ideal for mountain-biking in the summer and groomed for cross-country skiing in the winter.
- Bancroft is home to the North Hastings Heritage Museum, an art gallery and a geology museum, all located on Station Street at the site of the town's former railroad station. The Heritage Museum houses farming and logging implements, and antique furnishings and household items, most of them donated by people whose families helped to settle the North Hastings area over a century ago. The Mineral Museum exhibits an impressive collection of rocks and minerals. It also sells guidebooks, maps and permits for field trips to local mineral sites during the summer. The Bancroft Gemboree, held every year in early August, attracts rockhounds from far and wide to its gem and mineral show.

Practical Information

Silent Lake Provincial Park

- Park Season: open all year.
- Park Permit: required for all Silent Lake Park users, available from the office at the park entrance.
- Camping: Silent Lake has a well-serviced campground with 167 sites. Ten of these sites are electrical and 34 are walk-in sites adjacent to the lake. They should be reserved in advance during the busy summer months. In addition to the campsites, Silent Lake also has several yurts (spacious, tent-like structures, heated and supplied with basic furnishings) and a lodge for more luxurious accommodation.

- Information: park office (613) 339-2807, Ontario Parks Reservation Service 1-888-668-7275, www.ontarioparks.com.

Maps & Publications
- A guide to the trails of Silent Lake Provincial Park, containing maps and information about the park's hiking, biking and ski trails, is available from the park office.
- Silent Lake, together with the adjacent land and lakes, is covered by the NTS topographic map for Gooderham (#31-D/16).

Supplies & Accommodations Outside the Park
- Supplies and accommodations are available in the towns of Bancroft, 23 km to the north of Silent Lake, or Apsley, 20 km to the south.
- Bancroft area tourism information is available from the Bancroft & District Chamber of Commerce at (613) 332-1513, www.commerce.bancroft.on.ca.

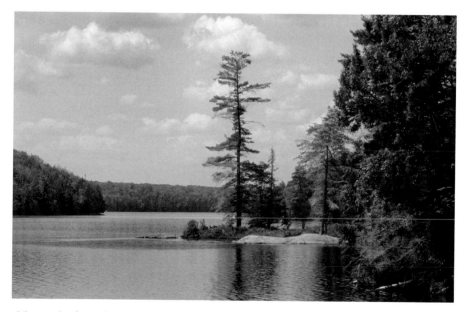

Silent Lake from the Lakeshore Trail

Chapter 5

Petroglyphs

Overview

Petroglyphs Provincial Park is located in the Kawarthas, about half way between Peterborough and Bancroft. The park was established in 1976 to protect one of North America's largest and most sophisticated collections of Native rock carvings. The carvings were created by Algonkian-speaking people 600 to 1100 years ago, but remained in relative obscurity until the mid 1900s, when roads gradually opened the area to travel by non-Natives. They were "discovered" in 1954 by two mining prospectors, whose reports kindled wide public interest. In subsequent decades, researchers have examined the petroglyphs and identified some 900 carvings. The images included creatures from the natural world, human figures with their boats and tools, and representations of Native spirits. Researchers also found that erosion, both by natural forces and by acid rain, was causing serious deterioration in the carvings, so in 1984 a building was constructed over the site to protect them. (For a more detailed discussion of the images see *Petroglyphs and Pictographs*, page 42.)

The rock into which the petroglyphs are carved is an outcropping of marble — metamorphosed limestone, formed originally from the accumulated shells of sea creatures. It is a soft, porous rock that is easily eroded. Water has sculpted holes and curiously shaped fissures in the outcrop, and the Native craftspeople incorporated many of these geological features into their carvings: snakes slither out of one crevice and into another, and eyes peer from holes.

Although the main focus of Petroglyphs Provincial Park is naturally its petroglyphs, the park, together with the adjacent Peterborough Crown Game Reserve, encompasses a large parcel of land roughly 10 km across and 12 km from north to south. Within this area are several hiking trails, numerous small lakes and wetlands, and Eels Creek, which forms the west boundary of the Game Reserve. Visitors therefore may enjoy both a fascinating glimpse into Native culture, as well as the exhilaration of hiking and paddling in the Canadian Shield wilderness.

Eels Creek tumbling over High Falls

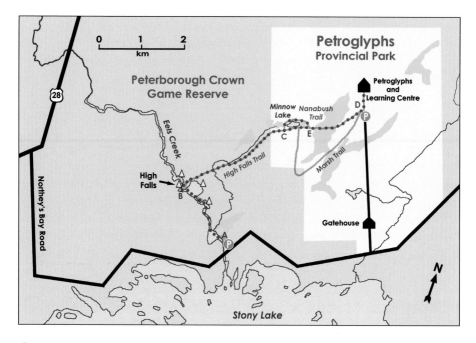

Access

- Take Hwy 28 north 37 km from Peterborough or south 62 km from Bancroft.
- Exit onto Northey's Bay Road (on the right when coming from the south, left when coming from the north) in the tiny community of Woodview.
- Follow Northey's Bay Road for 8 km to the bridge over Eels Creek.
- Cross the bridge and turn immediately left into a gravel parking area.
- Carry your boat 100 metres upstream from the parking area to bypass a small section of rapids, and put in at the quiet water above.

Eels Creek and the Petroglyphs

This excursion combines a pleasing variety of features, both natural and human, in a relatively short distance. Beginning and ending with an easy paddle along a peaceful river, and hiking a comfortable trail through magnificent Canadian Shield terrain in between, the excursion visits an attractive waterfall, a charming lake, an impressive wetland and, of course, the famous petroglyphs.

- Main Route: 11.5 km hike, 4 km paddle, 50 m portage(s)
- Alternate(s): 1–11.5 km hike

Route Description
1st Segment: Eels Creek to High Falls (2 km paddle, 25 m portage)
From the put-in **A** paddle upstream along the meandering course of Eels Creek. The creek is wide and placid for much of the distance, except for a small section of rapids about two-thirds of the way along, where a short portage is necessary. There is a bulge in the creek above the rapids, and then the channel narrows again, bends sharply to the right, and arrives suddenly at the base of High Falls **B**. The waterfall is a raging torrent during the spring run-off, but even in low water it produces a pretty cascade down the rock face. Pull your kayak or canoe ashore on the right-hand side of the falls and continue on foot.

2nd Segment: High Falls to Petroglyphs Provincial Park Trailhead (5 km hike)
Clamber up the rock outcrop to the top of the falls, turn right and cross to the eastern edge of the outcrop. A blue marker is tacked to a tree there, and the well-worn trail should be obvious. Near the beginning of the trail, where the ground is often muddy (or even submerged!) in the spring, the path forks twice; take the left-hand fork both times. The trail then continues along a ridge of rock in a fairly straight, northeasterly line for several kilometres until it reaches the "Provincial Park Boundary" sign. The ridge is pleasantly airy and open. There are many beautiful pines along the route, and underfoot the rock is carpeted with lichens and grasses. The trail alternates between rock and sand, and where it dips to cross damp areas, bridges and boardwalks have been built to make the passage easier. Shortly after the park boundary sign the High Falls Trail meets the Nanabush Trail (red markers) **C** and then the Marsh Trail (yellow markers). At each junction take the main trail to the petroglyphs; convenient maps on posts give directions. The trail hugs the south shore of Minnow Lake, and then traverses a boardwalk across a large marshland. On the other side of the boardwalk the ground rises gradually for the last kilometre of the trail, which ends at a gravel area with a large signpost **D**.

3rd Segment: The Petroglyphs (0.5 km hike)
Turn left at the signpost and follow the gravel walkway to the petroglyphs site. The walkway comes first to a grey wooden building called the Learning Centre, which was opened in 2002. The building contains the park office and store, where information is available and snacks, books and souvenirs may be purchased. The main purpose of the Learning Centre, however, is to introduce the visitor to some fundamental Native teachings about the world and the place of humans and animals in it.

A stroll through the Centre, with its contemplative atmosphere, its

Rock outcrop at High Falls

beautiful photographs and thought-provoking panels, sets the appropriate mood for the final stop on the walkway — the 10-metre-high glass-sided structure that houses the petroglyphs themselves. Inside, a deck encircles the rock outcrop, protecting the carvings from damage and giving visitors an elevated perspective from which to view them. A pamphlet giving useful information and offering interpretations of some of the images is available at the entrance. To Native peoples the petroglyphs are sacred "Teaching Rocks" (Kinoomaagewaabkong). Ceremonies are still conducted at the site, and offerings are left on the rocks. Native people from the nearby Curve Lake First Nation, the designated caretakers of the site, work alongside Ontario Parks employees to ensure that the petroglyphs are treated with proper respect, both spiritual and scientific. It should be noted in this context that, for Natives, the rock is a living body containing a spirit world, and because cameras steal and thereby diminish the spirit within the rock, visitors may not take photographs of the carvings.

4th Segment: Return via Minnow Lake to High Falls (6 km hike)
From the petroglyphs site, return along the gravel path to the trailhead signpost **D**, and then along the outbound trail for 1.5 km to the Nanabush

Trail junction **E**. Turn right and follow the Nanabush Trail, which skirts the marshy eastern end of Minnow Lake and then climbs to a rocky hilltop overlooking the north side of the lake. This makes an excellent place for a picnic lunch. Continue to the lake's western end, and, where the Nanabush Trail meets the High Falls Trail again **C**, turn right. Follow the High Falls Trail back to Eels Creek and your boat **B**.

5th Segment: Homeward from High Falls (2 km paddle, 25 m portage)
The final paddle is easy, travelling with the current. It may even be possible, depending on water levels, to run the rapids downstream and avoid the short portage.

Alternative: Omit the Paddle (1–11.5 km hike)
To limit the day's activities to visiting the petroglyphs and exploring some of the park's hiking trails, continue along Northey's Bay Road 4 km past Eels Creek to the official Petroglyphs Provincial Park entrance, obtain a permit from the gatehouse and leave your vehicle in one of the designated parking lots. The trails are well signposted and easy to follow from there.

Other Hiking Opportunities

The Marsh Trail (7 km, yellow blazes) is accessible from the main trailhead, and the West Day Use Trail (5 km, orange blazes) is accessible from the West Day Use area. Tiny McGinnis Lake, near the park entrance, is a protected

Petroglyphs building

glacial lake with rare, "meromictic " characteristics — distinctly stratified layers of water that never mix. A short walking trail visits the lake from the West Day Use area.

Practical Information

Petroglyphs Provincial Park
- Park Season: open for day use from early May to mid October.
- Park Permit: available from the gatehouse when entering the park by road.
- Camping: As Petroglyphs is a day-use park, no camping is available, but there are many private campgrounds within a short distance, and Silent Lake Provincial Park is only 40 km to the north.
- Information: park office (705) 877-2552, www.ontarioparks.com.

Eels Creek rapids

Maps & Publications

- The park's annual guide, available at the gatehouse and at the Learning Centre, contains general information about the park and a rough map of the hiking trails. The park's brochure about the rocks and carvings at the petroglyphs site is available at the entrance to the site.
- Topographic map #31-D/9 (Burleigh Falls) covers the Petroglyphs Provincial Park, Peterborough Crown Game Reserve and Eels Creek area at a 1:50,000 scale. It gives a general overview of the terrain but does not include the hiking trails.
- Note that, at the time of writing, there is a 6 km discrepancy between the park's guide and the topographic map with respect to the round-trip length of the High Falls trail. Fortunately the accurate distance is the topo's shorter one!

Supplies, Accommodations & Attractions Outside the Park

- Supplies and accommodations are available to the south at Burleigh Falls, Peterborough and Lakefield, all within 40 km of the park, or in Bancroft 62 km to the north.
- Backcountry paddle-in campsites can be found along Eels Creek in the Peterborough Crown Game Reserve. Being free of charge (to Canadian citizens) and easily accessible, these sites are vulnerable to overcrowding and abuse. Strict backcountry etiquette with respect to toilet habits and litter disposal must be observed if the integrity of the sites is to be maintained for future visitors.
- Information about accommodations, campgrounds and services in the area is available at Peterborough & the Kawarthas Tourism www.thekawarthas.net.

Chapter 6

Algonquin's Highway 60 Corridor

Algonquin Park hardly needs any introduction. Its landscape of rolling hills ablaze with autumn colour, its sparkling lakes, and its rocky shorelines are powerful Canadian symbols, immortalized in the paintings of the Group of Seven and recognized even by people outside the country. Established in 1893, it is one of Canada's oldest parks. It is also one of the country's most popular, attracting more than 300,000 visitors annually. This popularity can present a challenge for the wilderness enthusiast, as the park's campgrounds, lakes and hiking trails, especially in the accessible southwestern highlands region known as the "Highway 60 corridor," can at times be busy places.

The Algonquin highland landscape is characterized by steep, rounded hills interspersed with lowland lakes and marshlands. Its high elevation relative to the surrounding countryside gives it a cooler, moister climate. Five major Ontario rivers have their headwaters here. The soil covering is a comparatively rich mixture of sediment deposited by glaciers thousands of years ago, and well drained due to the hilly topography. This combination of physical features enables the land to support a great assortment of vegetation. Southern deciduous trees, 60–70% of which are sugar maples, blanket the hillsides. Pine trees perch on sunny cliffs and rocky promontories. And more northerly species like black spruce and tamarack — species able to tolerate a saturated, nutrient-starved environment — make their home in the lowland areas.

Algonquin's inaccessibility protected it from human encroachment well into the 1800s. But by mid-century the lumber industry had reached the highland forests. And by the end of the century when the park was created, most of the pine had been taken, and the paraphernalia of the log-drive — chutes, dams, booms and lumber camps — were scattered along the waterways. The railway line through the park (opened in 1897) and the highway (completed in 1936) gradually replaced the rivers as the means of transport for timber. Logging continues in the park today, but it is strictly managed

Rock Lake cliffs (photo by David Stone)

by the Ministry of Natural Resources and is now carried out by the Algonquin Forestry Authority, a Crown corporation formed in 1974 to replace the 20 independent companies that had operated in the parkland previously. Algonquin's logging history is admirably showcased at the Algonquin Logging Museum just inside the park's East Gate.

Hunting and trapping were other important aspects of Algonquin's early history. Park rangers themselves, in the line of duty, trapped fur-bearing animals to be sold at auction in Toronto, and were responsible for apprehending poachers in the park. "Poachers" included not only people but also wolves, which, in the early decades of the 1900s, were viewed as verminous predators. They were actively exterminated by rangers, who brought in 50 to 60 wolf carcasses every year. A shift in public attitude toward mid-century saw the abandonment of fur trapping by rangers. In 1958 a wolf research program was started, and in subsequent years the park's wolf population was increasingly protected. Algonquin's first Public Wolf Howl was held in August 1963, and it has since become an annual event, carefully orchestrated by park officials and attracting thousands of visitors.

When Algonquin Park was created, one of its main purposes was to provide people from populous centres with a place for recreation in a wilderness setting. Overcrowding was simply unimaginable in 1893! There were no reliable roads, and railway construction was only just beginning. To give visitors access to the park and an incentive to use it, parkland leases were introduced in 1905. Hundreds of cottages, many camps and thirteen lodges were built on leased properties along the railway corridor in the following two decades. And in the two decades after that, with the opening (in 1936) and the paving (in 1948) of Highway 60, the park became increasingly accessible and more widely used.

Around mid-century, the same shift in public attitude that brought protection to the wolves also changed visitors' appreciation of the park— away from recreation toward conservation, and away from fashionable resorts toward the more spartan pleasures of camping. The first camp-grounds were constructed at Tea Lake and Lake of Two Rivers, and interior campsites were set up along canoe routes and backpacking trails. Park authorities also began to phase out the cottage and commercial leases. Beginning in 1954 no new leases were issued and existing leases were permitted to expire. The Ontario Government purchased buildings within the park (including the Barclay Estate and Highland Inn, visited in this chapter's excursions) in order to dismantle the structures and return the land to its natural state. When this new policy was introduced, the leases were intended to be phased out by 1996, but the timing has been amended several times and many leases now extend to 2017. Even the movements of wilderness lovers themselves have become regulated to prevent congestion and preserve the park's wild spaces, with a quota system for backcountry paddling and hiking, and a reservation system for camping, instituted in the last decades of the 1900s.

Algonquin Park was established to protect the area's forests, watersheds and wild creatures for future generations. Despite the changing public attitudes and priorities, and despite the considerable and often contradictory pressures brought to bear by economic interests, recreational users and conservationists, the park has been largely successful in its mandate. The farsighted people who in 1893 took action to safeguard the Algonquin landscape could not have foreseen its stunning popularity a century later. But today, while we are paddling and hiking and enjoying the magnificent scenery, or even when we are lined up at a portage or wishing for a bit more solitude along a trail, we should pause to remember those people and be grateful. After all, Algonquin deserves its popularity because it truly is a beautiful place.

Early morning mist on Rock Lake

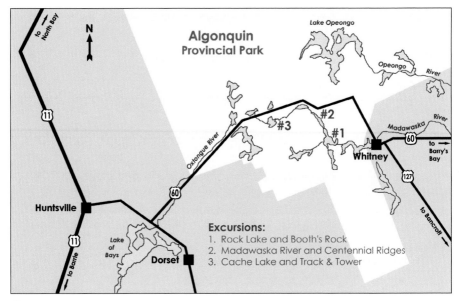

Access

- Approaching from the west, exit Hwy 11 at Huntsville onto Hwy 60 and follow it for 40 km to Algonguin's West Gate.
- Approaching from the east (Barry's Bay), take Hwy 60 for 50 km; or from Bancroft take Hwy 62 and 127 north for 60 km to the junction with Hwy 60 and turn left. Continue along Hwy 60 for 5 km past Whitney to Algonquin's East Gate.
- At the West and East Gates, information and park publications are available, and permits may be purchased for day-use or backcountry camping. If you are camping at one of Algonquin's drive-in campgrounds, pick up your permit at the entrance to the campground instead.
- Within the park, the 56 km of Hwy 60 are numbered from west to east and KM posts have been erected on the side of the highway for guidance. Continue from the West or the East Gate to the access KM for the excursions listed at the start of each section below.

Rock Lake and Booth's Rock

This is the gentlest of the three excursions described in this chapter, combining a 10 km paddle in Rock Lake with a 5 km hike along the well-worn Booth's Rock Trail. The route takes in many natural features, including two impressive cliffs — one on Rock Lake's southeastern shore, and the other atop the Booth's Rock lookout. It also pauses at several sites of human historical interest — Native pictographs on the western shore of

Rock Lake, the ruins of the once-magnificent Barclay Estate, and the railbed of the abandoned Ottawa–Arnprior–Parry Sound railway line.

• Main Route: 5 km hike, 10 km paddle

Access

- Exit Hwy 60 at KM 40.3 south onto the Rock Lake Road and continue for 8 km to the Rock Lake Campground office. Past the office take the first right-hand turn and drive 100 m to the end of the road. Leave the car in the parking area and launch your boat from the dock into the Madawaska River.

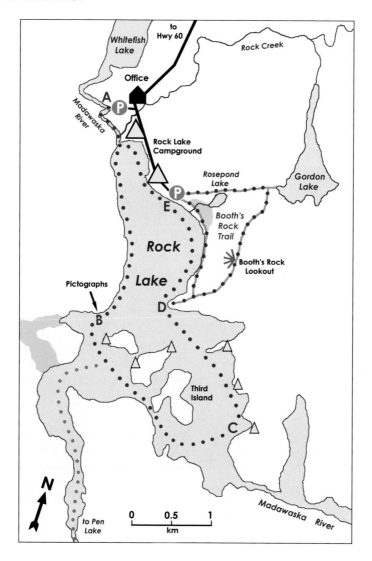

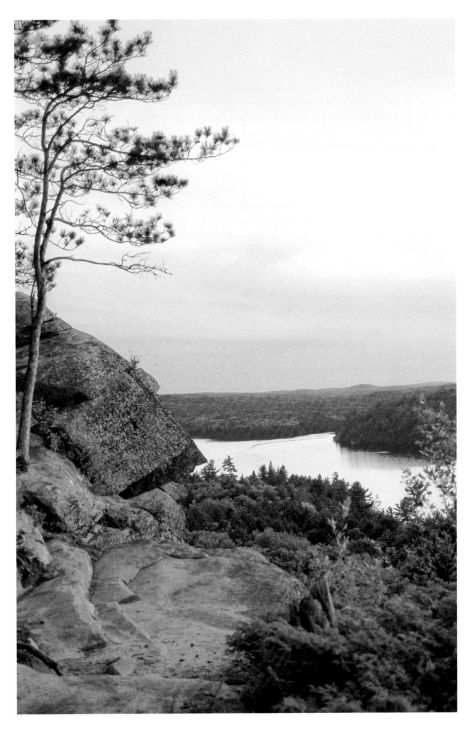

Booth's Rock Lookout

Route Description

1st Segment: Rock Lake Launch to Pictographs (4 km paddle)

From the launch A paddle downstream for 0.5 km into Rock Lake. Follow the right-hand shoreline of Rock Lake past half a dozen cottages. Partway down the lake the shoreline curves sharply to the west and a small cliff cuts into the lake B. Several red-ochre pictographs are visible on the rock face near the waterline here, painted by Native travellers centuries ago. The images are badly faded after years of erosion by weather and, sadly, from handling by subsequent paddlers.

2nd Segment: Pictographs to Rock Lake Cliff (3 km paddle)

From the pictographs continue south between the mainland and several picturesque islands. To the southwest, an arm of the lake takes paddlers over a 380 m portage into Pen Lake — worth exploring if time permits.

Back in Rock Lake, beyond Third Island the shoreline curves towards the southeast and an impressive cliff is visible on the opposite shore C. Cross the lake (where the Madawaska River continues toward Galeairy Lake) to admire the cliff's precipitous drop at close quarters.

3rd Segment: Rock Lake Cliff to Booth's Rock Trail (4 km paddle)

Turning away from the cliff, paddle up the east shore of Rock Lake past several small bays and backcountry campsites. At the tip of the largest point that juts into the lake D the cement foundations of the Barclay Estate dock can still be seen. The estate was built in the early 1900s by the family of J.R. Booth, a prominent lumber and railway magnate who had a tremendous influence on the human landscape of Algonquin Park in its early days. One of Booth's relatives, Judge George Barclay, inherited and augmented the estate property, which came to include a mansion, outbuildings, tennis courts, gardens, orchards, and the enormous dock on this point. The estate was last occupied as a summer residence in 1953 and was demolished in 1957 as part of the park's land reclamation policy. Paddle north 1.5 km beyond the estate. Just before the Rock Lake Campground there is a narrow sandy beach beside a small parking lot E, which marks the start of the Booth's Rock Trail. Leave your canoe or kayak on the beach here and continue on foot.

4th Segment: Booth's Rock Trail (5 km hike)

Pick up a copy of the Booth's Rock trail guide from the box at the trailhead. The sections of the guide correspond with numbered posts along the trail and discuss examples of the (generally deleterious!) effects of man on the park's environment. Follow the trail inland between the hills as it skirts

Rosepond Lake and then dips toward Gordon Lake. The trail is easy underfoot here — a track of sand and gravel with boardwalks over damp sections. Just before Gordon Lake the trail turns right and begins to climb, becoming rougher as the elevation increases. It emerges, a kilometre further along and 120 m higher, at the Booth's Rock lookout. The reward for the climb is a marvellous view westward across Rock Lake and beyond, over blankets of forested hills stretching toward the distant horizon.

The trail descends on the other side of the hill by means of a solid wooden staircase. It passes a jumble of enormous rocks at the base of the cliff, and then arrives at the entrance to the Barclay Estate property, which can be accessed by a short side-trail to the left. After strolling around the ruins of the estate, return to the main trail and follow it along the shoreline for 1.5 km to your boat. The flat gravel track you walk along is the railbed remaining from the railway line that once carried lumber, grain and passengers between Ottawa and Georgian Bay. This section of the line was closed in 1945 and the tracks were taken up in 1952.

5th Segment: Homeward (2 km paddle)

Paddle northwest along the shoreline of the Rock Lake Campground and back up the Madawaska River to the launching point A.

Madawaska River and Centennial Ridges

This is the most rugged and demanding of the three excursions in this chapter, with 13 km of paddling and 12 km of hiking, including climbs totalling 360 m. The paddling portion of the route follows the Madawaska River from Lake of Two Rivers to Whitefish Lake. The hiking portion takes you up to a series of rocky lookouts along two parallel ridges and visits several small lakes and wetlands in the low-lying areas between the ridges. The reward, on a clear day, is a magnificent view of the Algonquin landscape at its finest, and an exhilarating day's outing that will bring a solid night's sleep!

• Main Route: 12 km hike, 13 km paddle, 220 m portage(s)
• Alternative(s): 12 km hike, 7 km paddle

Access

• Exit Hwy 60 at KM 35.5 onto the East Beach road. Drive to the parking area at the end of the road and launch your kayak or canoe from the small beach into the Madawaska River.

Centennial Ridges Lookout

Route Description
1st Segment: East Beach to Whitefish Lake (3.5 km paddle, 110 m portage)
From the launch **A** paddle downstream along the Madawaska River. The river meanders placidly, flowing past the Pog Lake Campground. Keep close to the right-hand shoreline through this section to avoid losing your way in one of the arms of Pog Lake. At the southern end of the campground a short portage to the right is necessary to bypass a dam. Continue downstream past the dam for another 1.2 km, where the river empties into Whitefish Lake **B** at the Whitefish Group Campground.

2nd Segment: Whitefish Lake (3 km paddle)
Whitefish Lake is not much wider than the river at first, but it eventually opens into a broad expanse of water about 1 km across and more than 2 km long. The western shoreline (on the right) is low-lying and flat. Segments of the old Ottawa–Arnprior–Parry Sound railway bed, now a bicycle trail, are visible along its edge. The eastern shore, by contrast, rises steeply out of the water to magnificent rocky cliffs more than 150 m above the level of the lake. Keep close to this eastern shoreline, and pass between the mainland and a small island about one-third of the way down the lake. Just past the island, in a small bay on the left, a crumbling wooden dock juts out from a sandy beach **C**. Pull your boat onto the beach and lace up your boots for the hike that follows.

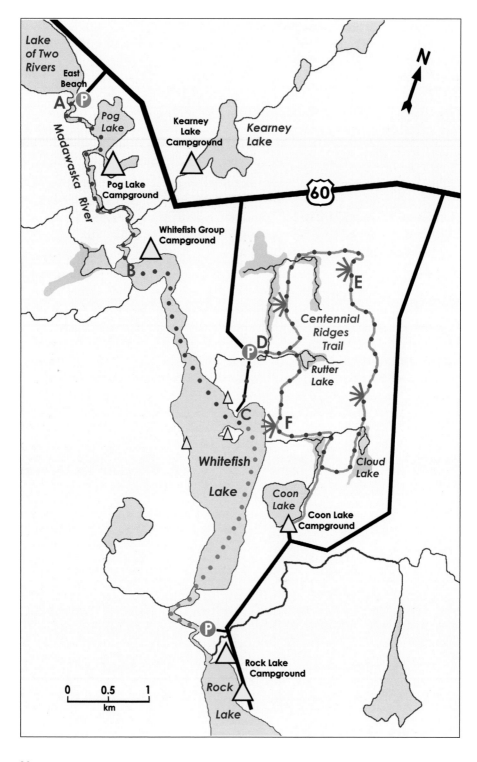

3rd Segment: Centennial Ridges Trail (11.5 km hike)

A convenient outhouse is perched in the grassy field behind the beach and a gravel roadway leads away to the north. Follow this road for 0.7 km to the Centennial Ridges Trail parking lot D. Pick up a guide from the box at the start of the trail. The 10 km Centennial Ridges Trail was opened in 1993 to celebrate the 100th anniversary of Algonquin Park. Fittingly, the trail guide takes the hiker to ten numbered posts in spectacular settings to celebrate the lives of ten people whose work was instrumental in the park's development.

The trail begins with a steep scramble past a small marshland and up the hill to lookouts along the first of two ridges. Turning east, away from the first ridge, the trail crosses a soggy lowland and climbs again through a forested valley to the second ridge — and to the highest point along the trail E, 170 m above the parking lot. Heading south, after another brief dip, another climb, and another ridgetop lookout, the trail descends to pretty little Cloud Lake. Then, curving back toward the west, it skirts a beaver meadow and climbs one last time to the most spectacular lookout of all F—the clifftop immediately above Whitefish Lake, which surely ranks as one of the most perfect picnic places in Algonquin Park! The trail is all downhill from here. At the parking lot D turn left and follow the gravel roadway back to the beach C, where a swim may be welcome before you set out on the homeward paddle.

Centennial Ridges from Whitefish Lake

4th Segment: Homeward (6.5 km paddle, 110 m portage)

Return north to the top of Whitefish Lake **B** and upstream along the Madawaska River to the East Beach A. After a long and strenuous day, it will be a welcome sight.

Alternative: Shorten the Paddle (12 km hike, 7 km paddle)

Use the Rock Lake access described in the Booth's Rock Excursion. Paddle north from the launch up the Madawaska River into Whitefish Lake and join the hiking segment of the excursion at the dock **C**. This access shortens the paddling portion of the excursion and omits the portages.

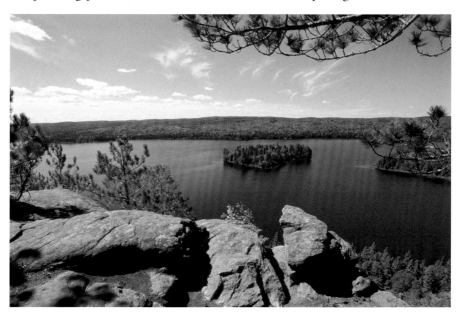

Whitefish Lake Lookout

Cache Lake and Track & Tower Trail

This excursion is steeped in the human history of Algonquin Park. Beginning at Cache Lake, once the hub of park activity, the route visits the site of a fire tower and a logging chute, and follows a track that was once a marvel of engineering that supported a busy railway line. Along the way, the route takes in many lovely natural features, including a clifftop lookout over Cache Lake and a rocky gorge through which the Madawaska River tumbles. With 8 km of paddling and 9 km of hiking, the excursion is not overly strenuous, although it can be expanded, almost indefinitely, by extending the paddle (and adding portages) down the Madawaska River.

• Main Route: 9 km hike, 8 km paddle
• Alternative(s): 4 km hike, 10+ km paddle, 550+ m portage(s)

Access

•   Exit Hwy 60 at KM 23.5 into the parking area for Cache Lake and Bartlett
    Lodge. Launch your kayak or canoe from the dock. (Note: Before setting
    out for the access point, pick up a copy of the Track & Tower trail guide,
    either from the East or the West Gate upon entry into the park, or from
    the trailhead at KM 25.0)

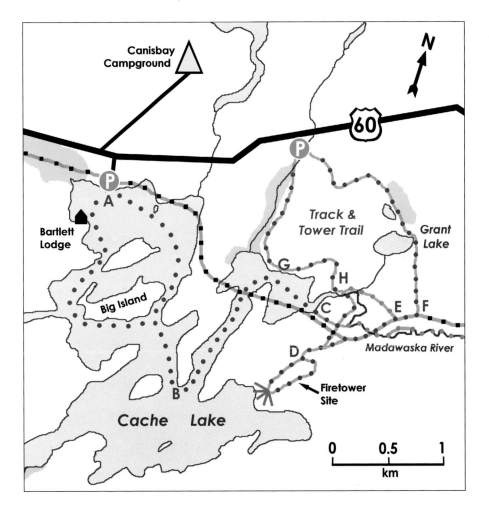

Route Description
1st Segment: Cache Lake to the Madawaska River (4 km paddle)

The Cache Lake launch, with its sturdy wooden dock, its parking lot and its outhouses and garbage containers, gives every appearance of solidity and permanence. These amenities, however, are of relatively recent construction. The site that they now occupy was once the heart of Algonquin, containing the Park Headquarters, the Algonquin railway station and the luxurious Highland Inn. The Park Headquarters, which in its later years even included a small airfield, was moved from its original location on Canoe Lake in 1897 and operated at Cache Lake until 1959 when it moved to the East Gate near Whitney. The railway station was a major stop on the Ottawa–Arnprior–Parry Sound railway line, first bringing visitors to Algonquin Park in the early 1900s before the highway was built. And Highland Inn, established in 1908, offered those early visitors to very sumptuous accommodation, including tennis courts, a dance pavilion, a games room and a boathouse. The inn was purchased by the Ontario Government in 1956 and demolished the following year according to the terms of the park's land reclamation policy.

From the launch **A** turn left and paddle along the shore of Cache Lake, first east and then south, to the tip of a peninsula where the unusual wooden buildings of Camp Northway-Wendigo can be seen **B**. Camp Northway was established at the site in 1908 — the first camp in Algonquin Park and the first girls' camp in Canada. Under the influence of its founder, Fannie Case, a teacher from Rochester, New York, it provided young women with character-developing experiences in a natural setting with few modern conveniences (the antithesis of the Highland Inn erected around the corner the same year!). Camp Wendigo was a later addition, begun in 1965 as a canoe-tripping base-camp for boys.

After rounding the camp peninsula, paddle north through a narrow channel. Near the top of the channel, take care not to run aground on a partly submerged wooden structure — the foundation of the Cache Lake trestles that once supported the Ottawa–Arnprior–Parry Sound railway line. The history of this railway begins in 1888 with the granting of a charter to lumberman and railway baron J.R. Booth, so that he could connect his Canadian Atlantic Railway line in the east with the ports of Georgian Bay to the west. The line was officially opened in 1897 and soon became one of the country's main transportation routes. Trains passed along it every 20 minutes, carrying timber from Algonquin to mills in more populous centres, and transporting Prairie grain from elevators along Georgian Bay to markets in the east. The line was costly to maintain, however, and the elaborate Cache Lake trestles were particularly troublesome. Meanwhile, the road that became Hwy 60 gradually took shape, offering an increasingly attractive alternative for passengers and freight traffic. Road construction began in 1933. That same year, the Cache Lake trestles were condemned. Over the next two decades, as the highway improved, the railway declined. The eastern section of railway from Cache Lake to Whitney was abandoned by 1945, and the tracks were taken up in 1952. The western section continued operating as far as the Cache Lake station until 1959, and then it, too, was removed. All that remains of the line today is the railbed, used by hikers and cyclists — and dogsledders in the winter.

Turn right where the lake opens up just beyond the trestles, and paddle to the far shore. Pull your boat ashore at the start of the Madawaska River portage C and continue on foot.

2nd Segment: Track & Tower Trail, Southern Loop (3 km hike)
A confusing maze of trails crisscrosses this area. Where the portage trail meets the hiking trail turn right, and keep turning right at each intersection. The trail climbs uphill, gradually at first, then steeply, with a welcome set of wooden stairs D to aid the final portion of the ascent. At the top, take the trail leading straight ahead, which soon passes the cement foundation of the Skymount fire tower. It was one in a network of eight towers used to guard Algonquin Park (and its valuable timber resources) before aerial surveillance replaced the tower system for forest fire detection. Just past the fire tower the trail emerges onto a rocky ledge overlooking Cache Lake, which makes a splendid picnic lunch spot. It then loops back to the stairs D. Down the hill turn right at the next two junctions, and follow the trail along the old railbed to the ruins of the railway bridge over the Madawaska River. A short distance up the hill on the other side of the river the trail comes to a junction E.

3rd Segment: Track & Tower Trail, Northern Loop (5 km hike)
Turn right, follow the track for 150 m to the next junction F, and turn left. This trail makes a large loop northward, skirting Grant Lake, winding through a maple forest, and then crossing the Track & Tower trailhead parking lot (where trail guides and an outhouse are available), before returning alongside a stream to the Cache Lake shore. At Post #2 G the disintegrating railway trestles are visible across the lake, and underfoot can be seen the remnants of a cottage property — one of those that were demolished under the land reclamation policy. After following the shoreline for 1 km the trail emerges into a clearing where water from Cache Lake pours over a dam on its way down the Madawaska River H.

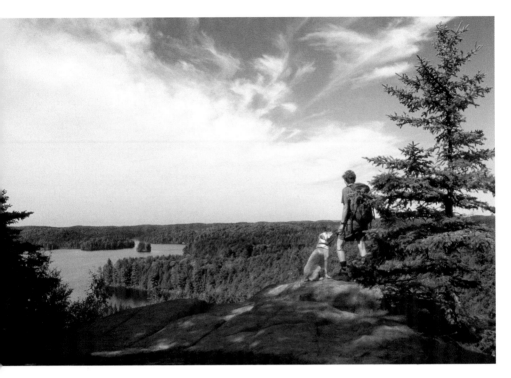

Cache Lake Lookout

4th Segment: Homeward (0.7 km hike, 4 km paddle)

A modern concrete structure controls the water level here now, but a century ago it was the site of a wooden dam and a logging chute. During the spring run-off, the chute was used to flush timber over the rocky section of the Madawaska River below. In the late 1800s there were dozens of such chutes scattered along the park waterways, but they fell into disuse during the early 1900s when the railway became the main means of transportation for logs.

Taking a brief break from the history lesson, the trail leaves the dam and crosses a footbridge over the Madawaska, following the river downstream through a magnificent rocky gorge. After several twists, the hiking trail meets the portage trail. Turn right and return along the portage your boat **C**. Retrace the route of the outward paddle, or for variety, paddle along the south side of Big Island and up Cache Lake's western shore instead. The shoreline is dotted with buildings — private cottages, and also Bartlett Lodge, which opened in 1923 and is one of the only three lodges remaining in the park. These modern buildings, and the motorboat traffic scurrying between them, bring the excursion abruptly back to the present during the paddle back to the launch **A**.

Alternative 1: Omit the Northern Hiking Loop (4 km hike, 8+ km paddle)

To shorten the hiking portion of the excursion, turn left instead of right at junction E and follow the trail west for 0.7 km to the dam H. This omits the 5 km northern loop of the Track & Tower Trail described in the 3rd segment of the excursion and picks the route up again at the 4th segment. Back at your boat, you could opt to paddle directly back to the launch A, spend more time exploring Cache Lake, or paddle down the Madawaska River (see Alternative 2).

Alternative 2: Lengthen the Paddle (4 km+ hike, 10+ km paddle, 550+ m portages)

To extend the paddling portion of the excursion, carry your boat over the portage C and paddle down the winding course of the Madawaska River as far as your time and energy will allow.

Other Paddling & Hiking Opportunities

The three excursions presented in this chapter, together with the Achray excursion in Chapter 3, merely scratch the surface of the possibilities that Algonquin Park offers. More than 60 books have been written about the park, as well as some 1,800 scientific papers, so there is no shortage of reference material. With 7653 km^2 of land, 140 km of backpacking trails, 16 short day-hiking trails, 2100 km of canoe routes and seemingly endless metres of portages, there is plenty of scope for adventure. Armed with a collection of maps and guidebooks, and a bit of imagination, the traveller can spend the winter planning excursions to last the rest of the season, and still have some left over for the next year!

Practical Information

Algonquin Provincial Park
- Park Season: open year-round.
- Park Permit: required for all Algonquin Park users, available from the East or West Gate.
- Camping: Algonquin's Hwy 60 corridor has 9 drive-in campgrounds containing more than 1,200 campsites. In the park interior there are almost 2,000 backcountry campsites scattered along Algonquin's lakes and backpacking trails. Accessible sites, both drive-in and backcountry, are in heavy demand during the summer months and on holiday week-ends, so it is advisable to use the park reservation service to book ahead.

The Mew Lake Campground is open year-round (with insulated toilet and shower facilities!), giving hardy visitors the opportunity for winter camping. Mew Lake also has seven yurts — spacious, tent-like structures that are heated and supplied with basic furnishings.

- A ban on cans and bottles is in effect in the Algonquin Park interior, which includes all lakes and day-use trails as well as backcountry campsites.
- Information: park office (705) 633-5572, Ontario Parks Reservation Service 1-888-668-7275, www.ontarioparks.com.
- Friends of Algonquin Park, a non-profit association, was formed in 1983 to assist Algonquin staff in raising funds and providing educational programs, facilities and publications for park visitors. They also operate the bookshops at the Visitor Centre and the Logging Museum. Information about the Friends is available on their website, www.algonquinpark.on.ca.

Maps & Publications

- As part of its Adventure Map series, Chrismar Mapping Services has produced several excellent waterproof topographic maps of the Algonquin Park area, complete with hiking trails, portages, campsites and many points of interest. The excursions in this chapter are covered by the 1:80,000 map *Algonquin 3: Corridor South*, which is available from Algonquin Park stores and from many outdoor stores across the province.
- The Friends of Algonquin Park have published maps for the park's canoe routes and backpacking trails, and have put together a splendid series of hiking trail guides and information booklets describing the natural features and human history of the park. These can be purchased at the East or West Gate, at the Visitor Centre at KM 43 and at the Logging Museum at KM 54.5. The maps are widely available at outdoor stores across the province, and the trail guides are also available in boxes at the trailheads.
- Algonquin Park publishes an annual Information Guide available at many locations in the park or upon request by mail. It offers up-to-date information about park fees, dates, regulations, facilities and activities. It also contains advertisements from local outfitters, supply shops and providers of accommodation.

Supplies, Accommodations & Attractions

- Basic supplies are available inside the park at the Portage Store (KM 14.1), the Two Rivers Store (KM 31.4), the Opeongo Store

(6 km north from KM 46.3), and at many locations along Hwy 60 outside the park.

- Within the park are three privately operated lodges: Bartlett Lodge on Cache Lake (KM 23.6), Killarney Lodge (KM 33.2), and Arowhon Pines (12 km north of KM 15). Other lodges, resorts and motels can be found just outside the park along Hwy 60.
- The Algonquin Visitor Centre at KM 43 was opened in 1993 to commemorate the 100th anniversary of the park. It has an excellent interpretive centre, a theatre, a restaurant and a giftshop.
- The Algonquin Logging Museum at KM 54.5, just inside the East Gate, has exhibits that explore this important aspect of the human history of the park.
- More extensive supplies and accommodations are available in the towns of Whitney to the east (5 km beyond the East Gate), or Dwight or Huntsville (25 km and 40 km respectively beyond the West Gate).

Chapter 7

The Frost Centre

The Leslie M. Frost Natural Resources Centre is a tract of Crown land nestled among the hills of the Haliburton Highlands. It is a large, irregular-shaped area more than 20 km across and 20 km from north to south. There are pockets of private land — mostly cottage properties — within its boundaries, and a main highway cuts across it. But the landscape of the Frost Centre is largely wilderness, and with dozens of lakes, several rivers and many miles of trails, it is a mecca for outdoor enthusiasts.

The natural character of the Frost Centre wilderness is pleasantly varied. Rolling hills are interspersed with barren rocky outcrops, craggy cliffs, steep valleys and boggy lowlands. The vegetation is similarly mixed. Hardwood forests blanket many of the hills, with abundant maples bursting into brilliant displays of colour in the fall. On rougher ground, where rocks are plentiful and soil is thin, hardy pines and blueberry bushes flourish.

Today the human character of the Haliburton Highlands is primarily recreational. Cottages, resorts and marinas dot the landscape, providing a playground for weary city-dwellers from the south. But it was the Highlands' vast timber resources, and in particular its massive stands of white pine, that originally opened the area to development. The first logging permit was issued in 1860, beginning a flow of timber — pine for the masts of sailing ships, and then lesser species such as hemlock for the construction of the Toronto subway system — that continued well into the next century.

Eventually the forests began to dwindle. Logging pressure was partly responsible, but forest fires were also to blame, and the Highlands' network of fire towers with their resident forest rangers was inadequate to combat them. So, forestry management became increasingly important. This led, in the early 1940s, to the establishment of a training facility at the Frost Centre site, where rangers could develop the skills necessary for forestry protection and development. Many of the centre's early students were soldiers, demobilized and unemployed after the Second World War. By the 1960s it had become one of Canada's pre-eminent forestry schools. After a brief hiatus at the end of the decade when the forestry education system was

Raven's Cliff

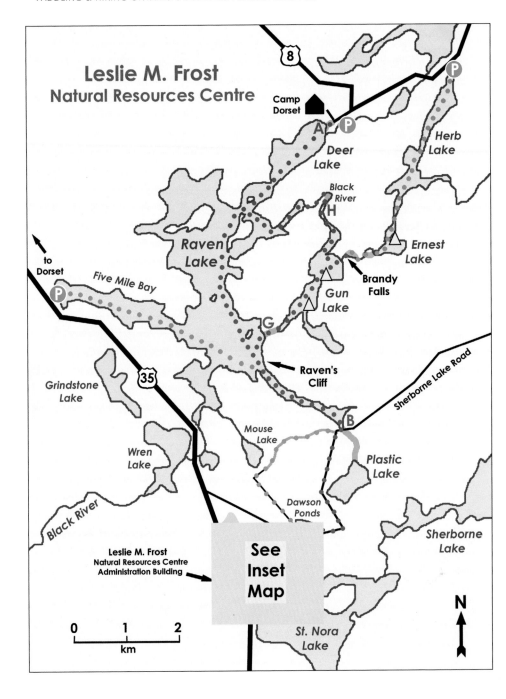

reorganized, the school reopened its doors in 1974 as an outdoor education centre with a complex of classrooms and dormitories on the north shore of St. Nora Lake and a program of courses for special-interest groups and the general public. It was christened the Leslie M. Frost Natural Resources Centre in honour of the late Ontario premier, a man dedicated to environmental issues.

Unfortunately, the Frost Centre's continued existence has been precariously dependent on government funding. Its education centre has now been closed and it faces the possible sale of its land to private interests. One can only hope that this swath of stunning Highland wilderness does not fall victim to political short-sightedness! Anyone interested in visiting the Frost Centre land should check ahead with the Ontario Ministry of Natural Resources for up-to-date information about accessibility.

Access

- Take Hwy 35 to Dorset.
- On the north side of Dorset, exit east onto Hwy 8 (Kawagama Lake Road) and follow it for 7 km.
- Turn right onto the gravel road at the Lion's Camp Dorset sign.
- Drive about 300 m to the point where the road forks, the main road turning sharply right toward the camp and a grassy track leading straight ahead.
- Just before this fork there is a small clearing on the left-hand side of the road where you may park your vehicle.
- Portage your boat 100 m down the grassy track to Deer Lake.

Raven Lake and the Geomorphology Hike

Geomorphology — the study of the landscape and the geophysical processes that shape it — is a guiding theme of this excursion. The hiking portion of the route follows several of the Frost Centre's trails, including its Geomorphology Hike, which gives a guided tour of local landforms and explains their origins. The paddling portion of the route provides additional examples of the area's geomorphology — an imposing cliff, a waterfall and a peaceful lake. Along the way, the route passes through some lovely Ontario landscape, so the excursion can be appreciated for its own sake, quite apart from its educational value!

- Main Route: 11 km hike, 14 km paddle, 520 m portage(s)
- Alternative(s): 11+ km hike, 0–19 km paddle, 0–980 m portage(s)

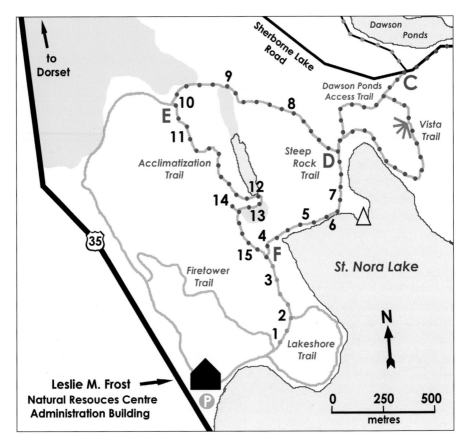

Route Description

1st Segment: Deer Lake and Raven Lake to the Plastic Lake Portage (7 km paddle)

From the launch **A** paddle the length of Deer Lake and through the narrows into Raven Lake. After crossing a shallow log-strewn area the lake opens up. Keep close to the left-hand shore and paddle southward to the opposite end of Raven Lake. The first section of this shoreline is sprinkled with cottages and small islands. But further south, at the point where the lake narrows, the contours change and cliffs rise dramatically out of the water. This is Raven's Cliff, a favourite nesting site for the bird for which it is named and once a place where Native people left offerings. Paddle along the edge of the cliff and down the narrow bay to its southern end. Leave your canoe or kayak pulled up on the tiny beach at the start of the Plastic Lake portage **B** and continue from here on foot.

2nd Segment: Plastic Lake Portage to the Frost Centre Trails (3 km hike)

Just a few metres up the hill, turn right onto the Sherborne Lake Road and follow it for about 3 km. The gravel road gives access to a few nearby cottages, but vehicle traffic is light and the road is generally quiet. After climbing over a hill, the road passes Plastic Lake on the left and then curves around Dawson Ponds on the right. Access to the Frost Centre trail system is just beyond Dawson Ponds, but the entrance can easily be missed. On the left-hand side of the Sherborne Lake Road, opposite a track leading to Mouse Lake, there is an open area C marked by a Ministry of Natural Resources sign. About 25 m up the hill past this sign, a small rocky outcropping stretches across both sides of the road. Exit to the left across the outcropping, where a white trail-marker will be visible on a tree. This is the start of the Dawson Ponds Access Trail, and from here the path is easy to follow.

3rd Segment: Frost Centre Trails Loop (4.5 km hike)

Continue along the Dawson Ponds Access Trail (white markers) for 100 m to the Vista Trail junction and turn left. Follow the Vista Trail (blue markers) to a rocky hilltop lookout with a lovely view over St. Nora Lake. The trail then descends through deciduous woodland to rejoin the Dawson Ponds Access Trail near the bottom of the hill. Turn left and take the Dawson Ponds Trail to its end at the junction D with the Steep Rock Trail (green markers). Turn right and follow the trail to its northern junction E with the Acclimatization Trail (red markers). Turn left and continue along the Acclimatization Trail to the southern junction F, then left again onto the Steep Rock Trail, which hugs the cliffs along the shoreline of St. Nora Lake and then circles back to the Dawson Ponds Access Trail D. From here it is a short walk back uphill to the Sherborne Lake Road C.

The Frost Centre's Geomorphology Hike encompasses the Steep Rock–Acclimatization Trails loop described above. Because this excursion approaches the Geomorphology Hike from the north instead of from the trail's usual starting point in the south, it picks up the hike at its mid-way point, covering the latter half first, then looping around to take in the first half. A series of numbered posts will be seen along it, corresponding to descriptions in the former Geomorphology Hike interpretive booklet. With the closure of the Frost Centre administration office, this booklet is not currently available, so a brief summary of the essential points follows, in the order in which the posts appear in this excursion:

Post 8	Water is an important agent of change in the landscape. It erodes the surface over which it flows and carries eroded material downstream, depositing it in other locations. The extent to which water is able to change the landscape depends on the nature of that surface. A soft surface of soil or sand is easily eroded. At this post, however, the surface is hard metamorphic bedrock, on which the small stream is making very little impression.
Post 9	The steep cliff and narrow swamp seen at this post formed when stresses within the earth's crust created a north-south fracture, known as a fault, in the bedrock. Glaciers subsequently gouged out the loose, crumbly material along the fault edge, and the resulting depression filled up with water and became a swamp. The dense rock on the eastern edge of the fault resisted the glacier's erosive power, so cliffs were left behind. And the crumbly material was carried from the fault by glacial ice, and will be seen at other posts further to the south.
Post 10	Although human technology can change the natural landscape out of all recognition, there are other ways in which the landscape shapes human activity. Roadways in the Haliburton Highlands, from the largest highways to the smallest trails such as those seen here, typically twist and climb to circumvent landform features. This is in marked contrast with the grid-shaped system of roadways in southern Ontario, where the gentler landscape is more easily subdued.
Post 11	This small area of blow-down illustrates the difficulty that trees have in colonizing the landscape of the Canadian Shield. Thin soil spread unevenly over dense bedrock provides a tenuous existence at best. The soil is unable to hold much moisture or sufficient nutrients to sustain trees as they grow, and because the root systems are small and shallow, the trees are inadequately anchored and easily toppled by wind.
Post 12	This post looks out, from a different perspective, over the swamp and cliff whose origins were explained at Post #9. An attractive view like this, and the more dramatic views found in mountainous or desert or arctic areas, can all be explained by geological forces.

Post 13	The small wetland seen from this post is full of peat. Peat is an accumulation of organic matter that forms when debris from dead plants is deposited at a rate faster than environmental bacteria can break it down. This typically happens in saturated areas with poor drainage, low oxygen levels and acidic, nutrient-poor conditions. Peat has accumulated in this wetland to a depth of four metres.
Post 14	The sparkling rock seen at this post is called pegmatite. It is an igneous rock, in contrast with the surrounding rock, which is metamorphic. It formed when cracks developed in the bedrock and magma from deep within the Earth seeped upward to fill the spaces. The magma cooled slowly and solidified to create large crystals of quartz (white) and feldspar (pink) that are characteristic of pegmatite.
Post 15	This is the last post for the Geomorphology Hike as it is typically approached from the Frost Centre complex to the south. It encourages hikers to stop and examine the landforms encountered along a trail and to contemplate the "why?" of a beautiful landscape.
Post 4	This tiny stream drains the swampland to the north. It has eroded small particles of sand and clay from the land over which it flows, carried them southward and deposited them in St. Nora Lake. But it is not powerful enough to move the larger rocks and boulders, which can be seen in the stream-bed at this post.
Post 5	The texture, shape and colouring of this rock tell the story of its formation. About 2.5 billion years ago sediments deposited by ancient rivers were compressed beneath the weight of subsequent deposits and turned into sandstone. Additional downward compression turned the sandstone into metamorphic rock with its minerals aligned into layers. Subsequent horizontal compression, caused by movement of the Earth's crust, folded the rock and made the layers twisted and wavy.
Post 6	A lake, like St. Nora Lake seen at this post, forms when water fills a natural depression in the landscape. Depressions in the Canadian Shield landscape were created by the actions of glaciers tens of thousands of years ago. Glaciers gouged away rock from weak areas in the Earth's crust — areas along fault lines (Post 9) and

Post 6 cont.	layers in the metamorphic rock (Post 5). Subsequent erosion by glacial meltwater and rainwater have continued the task, producing the pattern of lakes seen in the landscape today.
Post 7	The dampness that is typically seen at this post can be explained by the nature of the underlying metamorphic bedrock, which is dense and non-porous. When water percolating through the thin soil on the uphill side meets the exposed slab of rock, it builds up until it flows over the edge and trickles down the rock face until it is absorbed by soil on the downhill side. This gives the appearance, at times, of water flowing uphill across the rock.
Posts 1–3	Posts 3, 2 and 1 can be visited by making a short detour south along the Acclimatization Trail from the Steep Rock Trail junction F. At Post 3 the ground is composed of glacial till — a mixture of rocks, gravel and sediment. The mixture is unsorted with respect to size, as glaciers simply pick up all material from weak sections of rock (Post 9, for instance) and deposit it elsewhere. This contrasts with the action of rivers, which sort materials, picking up light sediments and carrying them great distances, and moving larger rocks for only short distances. At Post 2 glacial floats (large, boulder-sized rocks) are introduced. Like glacial till, floats (also known as erratics) were picked up and transported by glaciers, sometimes hundreds of kilometres from their original source. Post 1, the first post when approached from the trail's usual starting point in the south, introduces the hiker to a characteristic feature of the Shield landscape — an outcropping. Outcroppings are sections of ancient bedrock, formed deep within the Earth's crust, that have become exposed by uplift or erosion at the surface of the Earth. The rock underfoot at this post is about 950 million years old.

4th Segment: Return to Plastic Lake Portage (3–3.5 km hike)

Return to your boat along the outward route via the Sherborne Lake Road, or, for a slightly longer variation, turn left at C onto the Mouse Lake track. After 1.5 km the track curves right and passes several cabins on the shore of the lake. It then deteriorates into a rough trail and cuts over a wooded headland to rejoin the Sherborne Lake Road just before the Plastic Lake portage B.

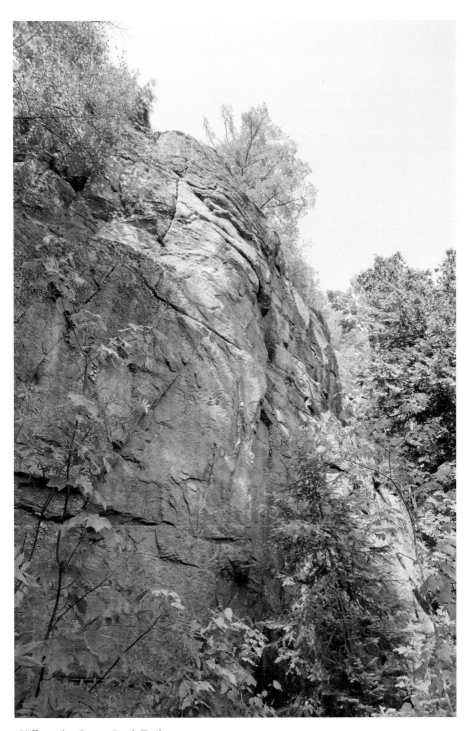

Cliff on the Steep Rock Trail

5th Segment: Homeward via Gun Lake and Black River (7 km paddle, 520 m portage)

Paddle back up the narrow bay beside Raven's Cliff. Having learned something about the landscape during the Geomorphology Hike, you can now see the cliff as the edge of a fault line in the bedrock. Keep close to the cliffside shoreline when Raven Lake opens up. Just past the first cottage, a yellow sign on the right marks the start of the portage to Gun Lake G. The 360 m portage is easy — flat, with a boardwalk across boggy sections. Gun Lake is not accessible to motorboats, so on a busy summer weekend its tranquility is very welcome. From the portage, paddle northeast up Gun Lake. For a pretty detour two-thirds of the way along the right-hand shoreline, follow the Black River upstream for 100 m (possibly having to lift over the remnants of a beaver dam or two). There, Brandy Falls tumbles over a rocky shelf, making a pleasant rest-stop, and recalling one of the Geomorphology Hike's lessons — the resistance of tough metamorphic bedrock to the erosive power of water. Returning to Gun Lake from the falls, continue paddling to its northern end H and take the 160 m portage, which bypasses a section of rapids. The portage ends at a quiet stretch of the Black River. Paddle downstream into Raven Lake and cross the shallow bay to the narrows into Deer Lake. From here it is just a short paddle back to the launch.

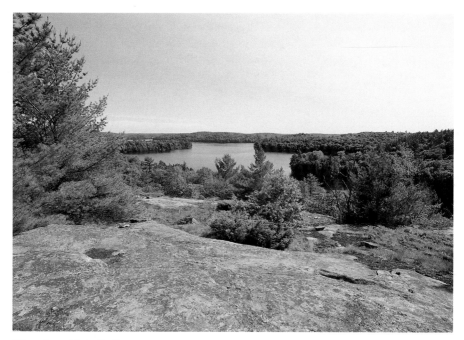

View from Vista Trail

Alternatives

There are many possible variations for this excursion. The Frost Centre's trail system consists of a series of loops, which can be hiked in many combinations. The paddling route can also be lengthened or shortened by putting in at alternative access points. Anyone armed with a map and the trail booklet can devise many splendid excursions there.

Alternative 1: Five Mile Bay Access

Put in at Five Mile Bay on the east side of Hwy 35 about 7.5 km north of the Frost Centre complex. Paddle southeast down Five Mile Bay and across Raven Lake to pick up the excursion at the base of Raven's Cliff. On the return, you may leave out the Gun Lake and Black River loop, reducing the total paddling length to 6 km each way and cutting out the portages altogether. As Five Mile Bay is a busy corridor for motorboat traffic into Raven Lake, this route is less peaceful for paddling. However, this approach allows more time for hiking the Frost Centre's trail system.

Alternative 2: Herb Lake Access

Put in at the north end of Herb Lake, about 2.5 km further east along Hwy 8 from the Lion's Camp Dorset road. The access road is marked with a yellow portage sign, but can be easily missed, and there is parking for only half a dozen vehicles. Paddle south down Herb Lake and Ernest Lake and into the Black River to join the excursion at Brandy Falls. This approach will lengthen the paddle by 2.5 km each way and add two short portages (170 m and 60 m) along the Black River, turning the excursion more appropriately into a weekend trip. There are several splendid backcountry campsites in Herb, Ernest and Gun lakes from which to explore the area.

Alternative 3: Frost Centre Access

To concentrate on hiking, park at the Frost Centre complex on the east side of Hwy 35 and follow the trail system from there. To the east there are 9 km of hiking trails, and across the highway to the west are 22 km of cross-country ski trails that hikers may use in the off-season. The Frost Centre complex gives direct access to St. Nora Lake for paddling, and by portage from there into other lakes.

Practical Information

Leslie M. Frost Natural Resources Centre
- Park Season: The Frost Centre land is open year-round. No permit or fee is required to use it. Unfortunately this can result in crowded

Brandy Falls

conditions on busy summer weekends, so backcountry etiquette is especially important in order to preserve the environment.

- Camping: Primitive paddle-in campsites with firepits and box toilets are available on the shores of many of the Frost Centre's lakes. Sites are marked with an orange sign, and there is no fee to use them.
- Information: Contact the Ontario Ministry of Natural Resources at 1-800-667-1940, www.mnr.gov.on.ca.

Maps & Publications

- Chrismar Mapping Services has published, as part of its Adventure Map series, an excellent waterproof 1:50,000 topographic map of the Frost Centre area, complete with hiking trails, portages, campsites and many points of interest. It is available from outdoor stores across the province and is a must for paddling and hiking in the park.

Supplies, Accommodations & Attractions Outside the Frost Centre

- Supplies and accommodations are available in the nearby town of Dorset. For information contact the Township of Algonquin Highlands at (705) 489-2379, www.dorset.muskoka-ontario.com.

- The Dorset Fire Tower is located in a pretty hilltop park just to the north of Dorset. The tower offers splendid views of the surrounding country side, and the park has picnic tables and toilets. It can be accessed by road from Hwy 35 or on foot along a short hiking trail that begins on Dorset's main street. Information, including park hours and a hiking trail map, can be found at (705) 766-2211, www.dorset-tower.com.

Black River below Brandy Falls

Chapter 8

The Massasauga

The Massasauga Provincial Park is situated in the heart of Georgian Bay's 30,000 Islands, just south of Parry Sound. It is a large park, encompassing discontinuous sections of mainland and inland lakes on its eastern side, and stretching on its western side into Georgian Bay to take in many windswept islands. The park began in 1969 as a small nature reserve on Moon Island, established to protect the natural environment that was rapidly vanishing in the path of cottage construction. In the decades that followed, additional properties were included and increasing protection was afforded by the granting of Provincial Park status, so that he Massasauga now covers an area of 130 km² and provides a sanctuary for such endangered species as the Massasauga rattlesnake, the five-lined skink and the prairie warbler. The park is accessible by water only. There are no recreation facilities, roads or campgrounds — just a wonderful collection of waterfront tent sites, and seemingly endless opportunities for paddling and hiking.

The landscape of Georgian Bay is famous for its smooth, weathered rocks that curve above the waters like giant whalebacks, with scattered pine trees clinging precariously to their surfaces. These are the roots of the ancient Grenville mountain range that formed 1.5 to 1 billion years ago when a group of small continents collided with each other and then rammed into an older continental mass to the northwest. During this collision, the Massasauga's rocks were buried as deeply as 30 km underground and subjected to intense pressure and high temperatures. The original rocks partially melted and then cooled slowly to form a dense, coarse-grained metamorphic rock called gneiss (pronounced "nice"). Pressure caused the crystals within the rock to realign themselves into multicoloured bands, folded and twisted into striking patterns. To further complicate their appearance, molten material seeped into cracks and solidified to form ribbons of igneous rock (typically granite, pegmatite and diabase), often at odd angles to the original metamorphic layers.

In the millennia after the formation of the Grenville range the mountains were levelled again, first by the scouring action of glacial ice and debris, and then by the massive flow of meltwater as the glaciers receded. So the rocks

The Massasauga rocky shoreline (photo by David Stone)

once buried at the roots of mountains were gradually exposed, smoothed and sculpted to become the beautiful rocky shoreline of the Massasauga, and the rugged home of the hardy plants and creatures that inhabit the park today.

Undoubtedly the most interesting of these creatures is the park's namesake. The Massasauga rattlesnake, Ontario's only venomous snake, is found in isolated pockets around Georgian Bay near Parry Sound and across the Bay on the Bruce Peninsula and Manitoulin Island. Its preferred habitat is marshland, but it may also be found in wooded uplands or sunning itself on exposed rocks. It is active from late April to early November, hibernating in rocky crevasses during the winter months. The snake is short (60–80 cm) and stocky with a triangular head, thin neck and blunt tail tipped with a segmented rattle. It is grey with brown patches along the back and sides, and its underside is dark. It has vertical eye pupils, heat-sensing pits between the eyes and nostrils with which it detects prey (typically small mammals), and fangs with which it injects its venom, a specialized digestive enzyme that disrupts the prey's blood-clotting system. It is shy and passive, with no interest in humans except to avoid them. Encounters with the snake are a rare and exciting privilege, but sensible precautions should be taken. Wear hiking boots and some sort of protective leg covering, ideally gaiters. Keep your eyes on the trail, put your hands only where you can see them, and keep your ears tuned for the warning buzz of a snake's rattle. The Massasauga's striking distance is just one-half its body length, so a bite is only possible when the hiker comes within 30 or 40cm – almost stepping on the snake! At far greater risk of snakebite is the curious nose of a dog, so keep your canine hiking companion on a very short leash!

Access

- From the south, take Hwy 400 north 85 km from Barrie to the MacTier exit #189. Follow Hwy 69 for 4 km to MacTier, turn left onto County Road 11 and continue for 6 km to the Healey Lake Road (on the left).
- From the north, take Hwy 400 south 24 km from Parry Sound to the airport exit #207. Turn left at the top of the exit, cross over Hwy 400, then turn right onto Hwy 69 South. At Gordon Bay, 8 km to the south, turn right onto Hwy 612 toward MacTier, and continue 4 km to the Healey Lake Road (on the right).
- Turn onto the Healey Lake Road and drive 16 km to the Pete's Place Access road, which exits on the right.
- Pete's Place Access has park information, trail guides, maps and souvenirs. It is also the registration office, parking and launch site for people camping at the park. Space at this location is restricted to campers only.

- For day-use purposes, continue 2 km past the Pete's Place Access road to Woods Bay, where parking and launch facilities are available, for a small fee, at one of the private marinas.

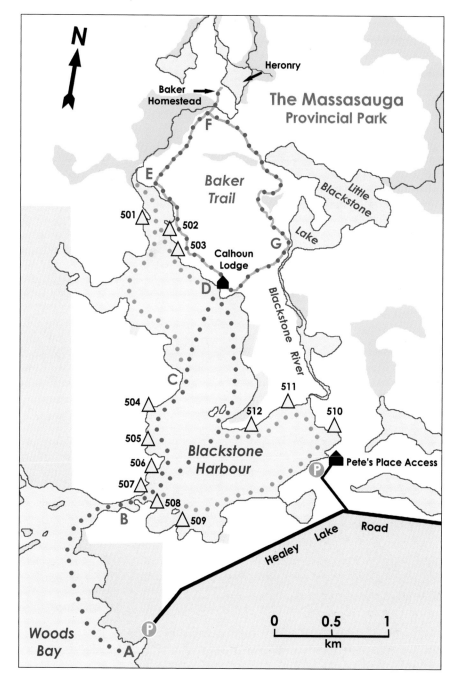

Calhoun Lodge

Blackstone Harbour and Baker Trail

This is a gentle route, combining an 8–13 km paddle in a relatively sheltered bay with a 6 km hike along a well-trodden and only occasionally rough trail. The focus of the route is the human history of the park, with visits to two historic sites, the restored Calhoun Lodge giving a taste of affluent cottage life in the mid-1900s, and the ruins of the Baker Homestead revealing the hardship of settlers earlier in the century. For detailed information about these sites, pick up a copy of the park brochure, *Calhoun Lodge and the Baker Homestead* at Pete's Place Access. The excursion also takes in some lovely rocky outcrops, a beaver meadow and a heronry.

• Main Route: 6 km hike, 8–13 km paddle

Route Description
1st Segment: Woods Bay to Calhoun Lodge (4–7 km paddle)
From the launch **A** paddle north for 1 km along Woods Bay, then through the narrows **B** into Blackstone Harbour. Follow the left-hand shoreline of Blackstone Harbour past several rocky campsites and around a steep headland **C**. For a longer paddle continue up the western shore to a marshy channel at the north end, then back down the eastern shore for 1.5 km. To take the direct route instead, paddle northeast across the harbour from the headland. Both routes lead to a small beach at Calhoun Lodge **D**. Pull your canoe or kayak ashore here and continue on foot.

2nd Segment: Baker Trail from Calhoun Lodge to the Baker Homestead (2.5 km hike)

Calhoun Lodge belonged to Joseph Calhoun, a lawyer from Cleveland, Ohio, who purchased the 300 acres of land along Blackstone Harbour in 1939. He first built the lodge and then added a collection of outbuildings — guest cabins, a caretaker's house, a kitchen building, several storage sheds, a barn, a boathouse, a generator building and a water tower — and also a hayfield and an extensive garden. The property was the Calhoun family's summer residence until Joseph Calhoun's death in 1972. The Crown purchased the land in 1974, and the buildings were restored in 1993 with the assistance of the Parry Sound Nature Club and donations of furnishings from local residents. The lodge, now a museum, is open to the public during the summer season.

Baker Trail begins behind the lodge. It follows the shoreline of Blackstone Harbour north for 1.2 km over rocky terrain scattered with oaks and pines. At the far end of the harbour the trail turns sharply right E, away from the water. About 50 m inland it passes two white wooden crosses (just off to the right of the trail) which mark the graves of Thomas Baker and his son Charles. They came to the area in the early 1900s when Charles was an infant, and set up a homestead (the next stop on this excursion) where they raised cattle and grew vegetables. Sadly, in 1932, Charles died at the age of 32 when he fell through the ice on nearby Gropp's Marsh. Thomas continued to work the farm for another decade. He died in 1944 and was buried beside his son.

From the gravesites the trail continues inland for another kilometre along the edge of a large beaver meadow. At the eastern end of the meadow take the left-hand fork F, which crosses a small creek and then climbs for several hundred metres over higher ground to the ruins of the Baker homestead. Although the setting is lovely, there is a melancholy air about the place, with rotting timber from the old buildings, rusting vehicle parts and overgrown fields bordered by piles of rocks — the few fragments remaining from the home of Thomas and Charles

Remnants of a barn at the Baker homestead

who laboured so hard to make a life for themselves in this unyielding country. The trail ends at a grassy ridge overlooking a beaver pond. The pond houses an extensive heron rookery, and their untidy stick nests can be seen in the branches of the dead trees across the water.

3rd Segment: Baker Trail from the Baker Homestead to Calhoun Lodge (3.5 km hike)

Return from the homestead site across the creek to the fork in the trail F and turn left. This part of the trail winds through a forested landscape of alternating hemlock and hardwood. The footing becomes rougher with many changes of direction, so take care not to lose the trail in all the ups and downs and zigs and zags. Little Blackstone Lake can be glimpsed occasionally through the trees to the left and comes into full view near the end of the trail, where a smooth rock outcropping slides into the water. A few metres past this outcrop the trail emerges at the end of the portage between Blackstone Harbour and Little Blackstone Lake G. Turn right and follow the portage for 730 m over the hill to Blackstone Harbour. Turn right again and scramble over the rocks to the beach at Calhoun Lodge D, where a swim may be welcome.

4th Segment: Homeward (4–6 km paddle)

From the beach, paddle south past several private cottages to a small peninsula with two pine-clad islands off its tip. The narrows can be seen across the harbour to the right, but for a longer paddle, continue around the peninsula to eastern end of the harbour, then loop back along the southern shore. The exploration of Blackstone Harbour complete, head through the narrows B to Woods Bay and turn left towards the launch A.

Georgian Bay & Wreck Island

This route is considerably more demanding, with a minimum of 24 km of paddling, much of it in the relatively open, wind-swept and busy waters of Georgian Bay. The 30,000 Islands bear the full brunt of the prevailing westerly winds sweeping across Georgian Bay, and can be battered by fierce storms. Paddlers must be vigilant, therefore, keeping a weather eye on wind conditions — and the other eye firmly on a good map — as one island can look alarmingly like another in the midst of 30,000! The 1.5 km hike along the Wreck Island interpretive trail gives a welcome leg-stretch in the middle of the long paddle. An excellent trail guide is available from Pete's Place Access, and (less reliably) from a box at the trailhead beside the Wreck Island dock. Though short, the trail can be challenging as it scrambles over rough terrain, dipping almost into the water in places during its exploration of the island's spectacular rock formations.

• Main Route: 1.5 km hike, 24 km paddle
• Alternative(s): 1.5 km hike, 30–32 km paddle

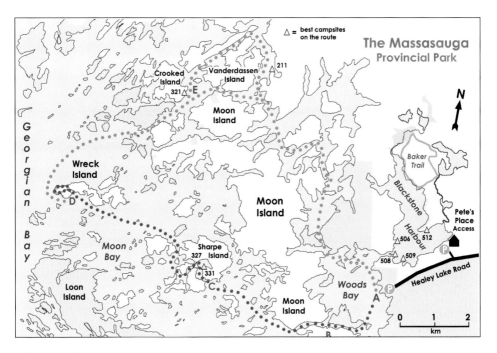

Route Description

1st Segment: Woods Bay to Wreck Island (12 km paddle)

From the launch A, paddle directly across Woods Bay to Captain Allen Strait B on the south side of Moon Island. Once through the strait, bear northwest. From here the route to Wreck Island is a maze of possibilities, with dozens of small islands to weave among, some little more than rocky shoals, and some sporting fantastic cottages. The most direct route passes to the north of Sharpe Island, following the main boating channel. A more interesting route is via a narrow passage that cuts into the south side of Sharpe Island C, passes several lovely campsites, and then exits west into Moon Bay. The paddling becomes rougher as you approach Wreck Island and the open expanse of Georgian Bay beyond. Tie your boat up at the day-use dock D in a small inlet on the island's southwest shore, where it can be left during the hike that follows.

2nd Segment: Wreck Island Interpretive Trail (1.5 km hike)

The interpretive trail crosses from the dock over to the north shore of Wreck Island, then hugs the shoreline closely around the island's western headland. Numbered posts along the route (marked by engraved rocks) correspond to entries in the trail guide. The trail stops at an echo rock, a giant clam, a rock that resembles a flaky dinner-roll, a percussion boulder abandoned by the glaciers, several pegmatite dikes, and many other features characteristic of the area's geology. It also looks at some of the island's plant inhabitants as it turns inland briefly on its way back to the dock.

3rd Segment: Homeward (12–20 km paddle)

Between the Wreck Island dock D and the launch at Woods Bay A lies the straggly expanse of Moon Island. The homeward journey, therefore, must either retrace the outward route through the Captain Allen Strait B to the south, or it must be extended into a large loop, passing to the north of Moon Island.

The northern alternative is at least 6 km longer, and for part of the distance it follows a main boating channel that can be disagreeably busy during the peak summer season. On more peaceful days, however, it adds pleasant variety and extra challenge to the excursion. From the Wreck Island dock, paddle around island's western headland, then northeast along the passage between Crooked Island and Moon Island. From 1913 to 1936 Crooked Island was a base for fire rangers who, armed with hand tools and pumps, patrolled the area's islands by canoe until they were supplanted by more sophisticated aerial surveillance systems. Now it is home to a splendid campsite instead. Beyond Crooked Island E you'll need to decide whether to follow the main boating channel to the right, or to loop around the quieter, but 2.5 km longer, northern side of Vanderdassen Island. The two routes

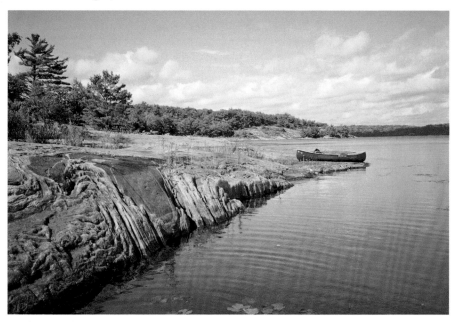

Rocky shoreline rest-stop at the Massasauga

converge again below Vanderdassen Island and continue along the winding passage down the eastern side of Moon Island. Eventually the passage opens into Woods Bay, and the launch A is just 2 km away — a welcome sight after a long day's paddle.

Other Paddling & Hiking Opportunities

Paddling:
- The Three Legged Lake access, located off Oastler Park Drive and Blue Lake Road, is the gateway to the northern side of the Massasauga. A 368 m portage from Three Legged Lake leads to a labyrinth of paddling possibilities in Spider Lake, Clear Lake, Spider Bay and beyond these sheltered waters into Georgian Bay. Day-use and backcountry camping permits for the Three Legged Lake access may be purchased at the nearby Oastler Lake Park office. With the proposed development of the Nipissing–North Arm hiking trail, this will become an excellent route for a future paddling and hiking excursion.

Hiking:
- The Nipissing–North Arm Orienteering Trail is a 30 km wilderness trail, marked but not cleared or maintained, which intended for map-and-compass hiking. The trail can be accessed from Devil's Elbow at the north-west corner of the park. Recent park publications have indicated that portions of the route will be developed in the coming years, making the trail accessible for general hiking.
- The Moon Island Trail is another proposed development, intended to extend in a 4 km loop from the Woods Bay picnic area around the south end of Moon Island.

[Note that, at the time of writing, these two trails are very much in the planning stage, so before setting out, interested visitors should contact the park directly for up-to-date information.]

Practical Information

The Massasauga Provincial Park
- Park Season: open from late April to late October.
- Park Permit: Backcountry camping permits are required for overnight use of the Massasauga Park and are available from Pete's Place Access in the south or from the Oastler Lake Park office in the north. Day-use permits are required for the Three-Legged Lake access in the north. As Pete's Place Access in the south does not have parking or launch

facilities for day-use visitors, day-use permits are not required for paddling and hiking in the southern part of the park.

- Camping: The Massasauga has 135 backcountry campsites, accessible only by boat, each with a tent pad, firepit and "thunderbox" privy. These sites should be booked in advance, as the prime locations near the access points are popular during summer weekends and holidays. Blackstone Harbour sites 501 to 512 are close to Pete's Place Access and to the Baker Trail. There are many sites on Moon Island, Sharpe Island and other small islands between Woods Bay and Wreck Island that provide suitable bases for these excursions. There is no drive-in campground at the park.

- Information: park office (705) 378-0685, Ontario Parks Reservation Service 1-888-668-7275, www.ontarioparks.com.

Maps & Publications

- The Massasauga Provincial Park has published an excellent topographic map at a scale of 1:20,000 — an essential companion when paddling and hiking in the park. It contains detailed information about paddling routes, portages, hiking trails, campsites and many points of interest in the park. It is available from Pete's Place Access, the Oastler Lake Park office and from many outdoor stores across the province.

- The park has also published interpretive trail guides for the Baker Trail and the Wreck Island Trail. These are often available in boxes at the start of the trails, but there are occasions when the boxes are empty so, to avoid disappointment, stop at Pete's Place Access to pick up guides ahead of time.

Supplies & Accommodations Outside the Park

- Basic supplies are available at Woods Bay marinas and at service stations on Hwy 69. The Massasauga Park staff are happy to provide names and telephone numbers of the local marinas.

- More extensive supplies and accommodations are available in the towns of Mactier, 6 km to the south of the Healey Lake Road, and Parry Sound, 36 km to the north. Parry Sound is a bustling place during the summer months, when its population swells to double its normal size with cottagers, tourists and music festival audiences. It has many shops and facilities to accommodate the influx. Parry Sound tourism information can be found at www.town.parry-sound.on.ca.

- Excellent outfitting services, boat rentals and boating supplies are available in Parry Sound from Massasauga Outfitters at (705) 746-8222 or White Squall at (705) 746-4936, www.whitesquall.com.

Information about the Massasauga Rattlesnake

- The Muskoka–Parry Sound Health Unit has put together some useful information about the rattlesnake, from a human health perspective, on its website www.mpshu.on.ca/environmentalhealth/rattlesn.htm.

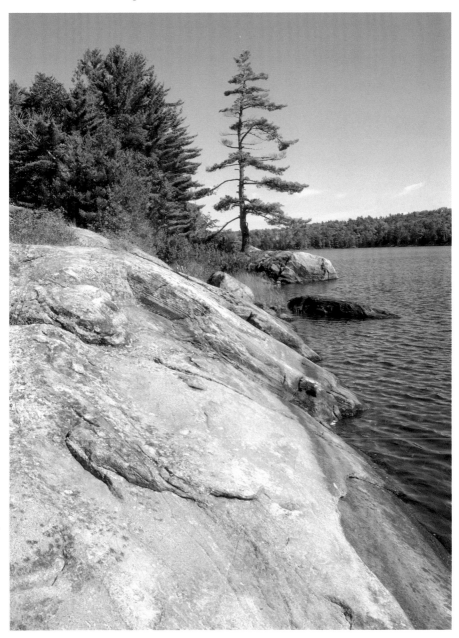

Rocky shoreline at the Massasauga (photo by David Stone)

Chapter 9

Grundy

Grundy Lake Provincial Park is located 12 km inland from the northeastern shore of Georgian Bay, roughly halfway between Parry Sound and Sudbury. It is a popular park with a large, well-serviced campground and several sandy beaches. It also has three short hiking trails, a camp store, an interpretive centre, an amphitheatre, and a lively program of nature talks and guided walks to introduce visitors to the park's natural history. Beyond this hub of activity in the southwest corner of the park, however, is the wilder side of Grundy, which is not so well known. It stretches for more than 10 km to the north and east along a string of small lakes and wetlands. Grundy's lakes are off-limits to motorboats, so are pleasantly peaceful. The park has developed a paddling route along these lakes, with portages between them. It has also constructed some paddle-in campsites, which, unfortunately, are not used as frequently as they deserve. For the backcountry enthusiast this presents a golden opportunity, as the sites make excellent bases from which to explore the more remote areas of the park.

Grundy's terrain is quintessential Canadian Shield. Knobbly outcrops of barren rock spread like ancient fingers across the landscape. Pine trees and lichens cling to their surfaces, and other hardy northern plants eke nourishment from thin pockets of soil along their edges. Between the rocky outcrops the lowland areas are filled with lakes and marshes. Reptiles and amphibians, aquatic mammals like beavers and otters, and many species of water birds are common in such wetlands. Paddlers who enjoy poking quietly along the shoreline are usually rewarded with sightings of some of these natural inhabitants.

Access
- Take Hwy 69 north from Parry Sound 78 km or from Sudbury south 85 km.
- Exit east onto Hwy 522.
- The entrance to Grundy Lake Park is on the left about 1 km from the turnoff onto Hwy 522.
- Stop at the park office and obtain a permit.

Gut Lake (photo by David Stone)

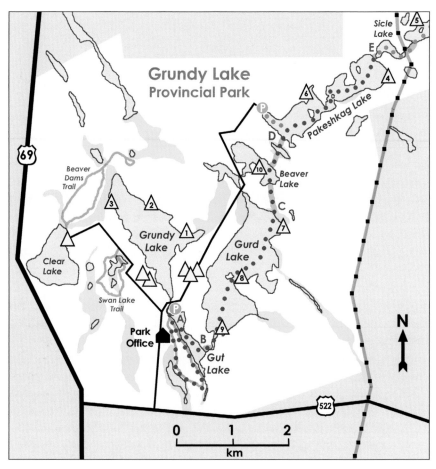

- Continue along the park road, which curves to the right and crosses Nisbet Creek. A few metres beyond the stream, take the exit on the right to Gut Lake, where there is a boat launch and a car parking area.

Gut Lake to Pakeshkag Lake

This excursion begins with a walk along one of Grundy's three short trails. The Gut Lake Trail introduces the hiker to the smooth rocky outcrops and the wetlands that are so characteristic of Canadian Shield landscape. The excursion then continues by boat over the park's chain of lakes to the north shore of Pakeshkag Lake, where water tumbles through a rocky channel on its way to the Pickerel River and out to Georgian Bay.

- Main Route: 2.5 km hike, 13 km paddle, 2000 m portage(s)
- Alternative: 2.5 km hike, 8.5 km paddle, 1000 m portage

Route Description
1st Segment: Gut Lake Trail (2.5 km hike)

From the parking area at the north end of Gut Lake, the trail crosses a footbridge over Nisbet Creek and follows the western shoreline of the lake. A series of interpretive signs has been set up along the trail to explain some of the geological features and introduce plant species that are typical of the area. A small, boulder-strewn stream flows from the south end of Gut Lake. The trail follows this stream briefly, then cuts west across a ribbon of highland. It returns northward along rocky cliffs overlooking a wetland, and loops back to the parking area.

2nd Segment: Gut Lake to Gurd Lake (1 km paddle, 330 m portage)

From the launch A paddle down Gut Lake to enjoy its beautiful rocks from the perspective of the water. The left-hand shoreline is lined with small cliffs — and often with adventurous young campers for whom it is a favourite jumping place. The rocks on the right-hand shoreline, by contrast, slide smoothly into the lake. Glaciers shaped this lake from a fault in the bedrock. They approached from the northeast, gouged debris from along the fault-line and dragged it over the rocks on the opposite side, wearing them smooth. When the ice retreated, the fault filled with water and Gut Lake was born. Near the south end of the lake, between the cliffs along the east side B, a portage sign marks the way to the next lake in the chain. The 330 m portage is not difficult — up a short rocky path, a right turn onto a sandy track and an easy walk to the marshy shallows at the south end of Gurd Lake.

3rd Segment: Gurd Lake (2.5 km paddle)

Paddle the length of Gurd Lake. The left-hand shoreline is a busy place, adjacent to the campground area and beaches, but the right-hand shoreline is wilder and quieter. Picnic Island, with its beautiful rocks and lonely pine trees, sits about one-third of the way along this shore. Continue to the northeast corner of the lake, where a portage sign guides the way through submerged logs and weeds to a boggy landing place C.

4th Segment: Gurd Lake to Pakeshkag Lake (1 km paddle, 670 m portage)

Portage 380 m over a height to Beaver Lake. There is a challengingly steep section near the beginning of this portage, but once you're at the top the trail is gentle underfoot and easy to follow. It ends at a pleasant pine-clad point in the southeast corner of Beaver Lake. Beaver Lake, being accessible only by portage, is a tranquil place for a brief paddle before you return to the northeast shore, where an easy 200 m portage takes you to a small unnamed

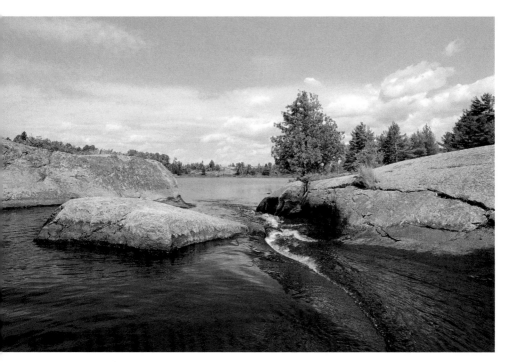

Pakeshkag Lake rapids

swamp. Paddle and pole across it and take the final, 90 m portage **D** to Pakeshkag Lake. The precipitous entry into the lake down steeply sloping smooth rocks requires careful footing.

5th Segment: Pakeshkag Lake (2 km paddle)
Pakeshkag Lake is long and thin, barely wider than a river in places, and is dotted with rocky islands and marshy areas. At the lake's northeastern end **E**, smooth bulging rocks form a barrier through which the lakewater tumbles on its way downstream to the Pickerel River. These rocks make a perfect place for a rest and a picnic before you begin the homeward journey.

6th Segment: Homeward (6.5 km paddle, 1000 m portage)
The return route is the reverse of the outward route, but the portages will feel longer on the way back!

Alternative: Car-Shuttle from Gut Lake to Pakeshkag Lake (2.5 km hike, 8.5 km paddle, 1000 m portage)
For a multi-person expedition with more than one vehicle, it is possible to avoid the long homeward journey and cut the number of portages in half by parking one of the cars at the end of the Pakeshkag Lake access road. This

twisty gravel road is a 3.5 km extension of the main park road which passes through the campgrounds between Gurd and Grundy lakes.

Paddling
Grundy Lake, the park's namesake at the top of Nisbet Creek, and Clear Lake, beside the Balsam campground area, give short paddling opportunities in the park. Longer paddling excursions beyond the park boundary at the northeastern end of Pakeshkag Lake can be accessed by portaging over the railway tracks and following the stream as it continues on its way to the Pickerel River and out to Georgian Bay.

Hiking
The Swan Lake Trail (1.5 km) and Beaver Dams Trail (3.6 km), each with an interpretive booklet, guide hikers through some of the park's wetland areas and introduce their natural features and inhabitants.

Rock outcrop along the Gut Lake Trail (photo by David Stone)

Paddlers on Gut Lake (photo by David Stone)

Practical Information

Grundy Lake Provincial Park

- Park Season: open from early May to the Canadian Thanksgiving weekend in mid-October.
- Park Permit: required for all users of Grundy Lake Park, available from the park office.
- Camping: Grundy has a large, well-serviced campground with 486 sites, 108 of which are electrical. Book in advance as they are popular, especially on weekends and holidays. The park also has 10 backcountry paddle-in campsites, which may be reserved in advance, though availability is not usually a problem.
- Information: park office (705) 383-2286, Ontario Parks Reservation Service 1-888-668-7275, www.ontarioparks.com.

Maps & Publications

- Grundy Lake Park has assembled a rudimentary map of the paddling route, with portages and backcountry campsites marked on it. Ask for a copy at the park office.

- Chrismar Mapping Services has published, as part of its Adventure Map series, an excellent waterproof 1:25,000 topographic map of the Grundy area, complete with hiking trails, portages, campsites and many points of interest. It is available at outdoor stores across the province and is a useful reference when hiking and paddling in the park.

Supplies, Accommodations & Attractions Outside the Park

- The Grundy Supply Post, just outside the park at the junction of Hwy 69 and Hwy 522, carries basic supplies, and offers canoe/kayak rentals. For information contact (705) 383-2251.
- The nearest large towns for more extensive supplies and accommodations are Parry Sound and Sudbury, nearly an hour's drive to the south and north respectively, so it is best to plan ahead when visiting Grundy.
- A visit to Sudbury makes an excellent rainy-day excursion while camping at Grundy. In addition to shopping and other useful facilities, the town boasts two excellent science centres — Science North, with displays and interactive exhibits about many facets of natural science, and Dynamic Earth, which concentrates on geology and mining, and includes underground tours of the Big Nickel Mine. For information contact (705) 522-3701, www.sciencenorth.on.ca or www.dynamicearth.ca.

Chapter 10

Killarney

Overview

Killarney Provincial Park is known affectionately as the "crown jewel" of Ontario's provincial parks system. Tucked into the northeastern corner of Georgian Bay, this parcel of wilderness boasts some of the province's most dazzling scenery. Accidents of geology have created a masterpiece here — the sparkling La Cloche Mountains, a ragged granite shoreline battered by storms off Georgian Bay, and a string of clear turquoise inland lakes and bubbling streams — attracting artists and outdoor enthusiasts for more than a century.

The accidents of geology that created the park landscape date back somewhat further — 2.5 billion years further in fact — when quartz-rich sediments were eroded from an ancient landmass to the north and washed into a shallow sea where Killarney now lies. The weight of successive layers compressed the sediments into sandstone. Then, during a shift in the Earth's crust about 2 billion years ago, the Grenville Province to the southeast rammed into the Southern Province to the northwest, subjecting the sandstone to such intense pressure and heat that it was transformed into the dense white metamorphic rock "orthoquartzite." Pressure from the collision also lifted the rock up into a massive mountain range rivalling today's Rockies. One and a half billion years ago, magma from deep inside the Earth seeped into the zone between the two geological provinces and solidified there, forming a coarse-grained reddish granite pluton. Other molten volcanic rock oozed into cracks in the quartzite and cooled to form dark ribbons of diabase. And finally, in the more recent history of the past 2 million years, ice ages scoured the land, grinding down the mountains and removing the overlying layers of rock to expose the mountain roots — the quartzite La Cloche hills and the pink granite ridges that make up Killarney Park today.

During the early decades of the 1900s the magnificent landscape of the La Cloche Mountains attracted members of the Ontario Society of Artists (OSA), including four of the famous Group of Seven — Frank Carmichael, Arthur Lismer, A.J. Casson and A.Y. Jackson — who captured enduring images of Killarney on canvas. These artists, and A.Y. Jackson in

Lone Pine on Killarney Ridge

particular, were instrumental in the creation of the park, actively lobbying government officials to protect the land from encroachment by the logging industry. In response, a small forest reserve was set aside in 1933. Continued pressure by artists and environmentalists prompted the enlargement of the protected lands in the 1950s. Provincial Park status was granted in 1964 and the boundary extended northward in 1983. Today Killarney Provincial Park encompasses 485 km² and is designated a Wilderness Park, giving paramount importance to protection of the natural environment.

Killarney suffered severely in the 1960s and 1970s from the effects of atmospheric pollution (for more information see Acid Rain in Killarney, page 152). In recent decades the natural environment has faced challenges from the sheer number of visitors who come to enjoy it. Like the park's famous sibling, Algonquin, Killarney's popularity has made it crowded at times, and strict regulations have been instituted to protect the park's fragile wild spaces. There are, however, few landscapes in the province that rival Killarney's natural beauty, and it entirely deserves its reputation as a "crown jewel."

Access

- Take Hwy 69 south 42 km from Sudbury or north 122 km from Parry Sound.
- Turn west onto Hwy 637. (Note: be sure that your vehicle has an adequate supply of gas, as the road ahead is long and the services minimal!)
- Follow Hwy 637 for 58 km to the Killarney Provincial Park office at the entrance to the George Lake campground.
- Purchase a permit from the park office.
- Proceed to the access listed at the start of each excursion.

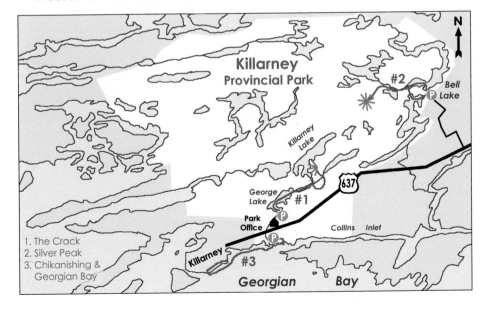

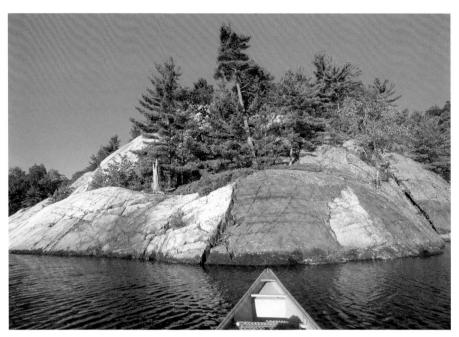

Quartzite with black diabase ribbons on George Lake

George–Freeland Lakes and "The Crack"

This excursion introduces the wonderful variety of Killarney's natural features—the white quartzite hills, the pink granite ridges, and the network of lakes and rivers that cuts across them. It travels the lengths of George and Freeland lakes to join the La Cloche Silhouette Trail for a climb through "The Crack" to the summit of the Killarney Ridge. With 7 km of hiking, 11 km of paddling and just one short portage each way, the route is not overly long. But the terrain can be challenging, with steep scrambles over jagged rocks in the hiking portion of the route, and an almost inevitable battle against the wind in the paddle down George and Freeland lakes. These difficulties are forgotten once you're up on the ridge, however, with Killarney and OSA lakes spreading out below and the La Cloche Mountains sparkling in the background—surely one of the most breathtaking vistas in the whole province!

• Main Route: 7 km hike, 11 km paddle, 100 m portage(s)

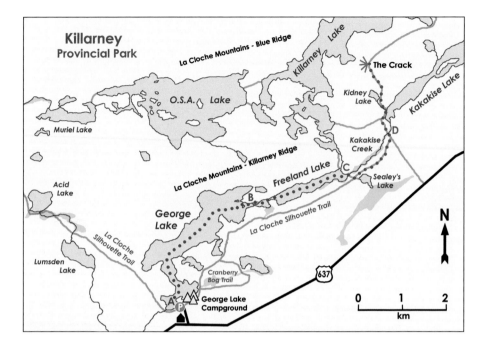

Access

- From the park office continue along the campground road to the main beach area, where there is a parking lot and a boat launch.

Route Description

1st Segment: George Lake to Freeland Lake (3.5 km paddle, 50 m portage)

From the launch **A** paddle north for 1 km through the channel into the main body of George Lake and turn right. George Lake fills a depression along the geological boundary between quartzite ridges to the north and granite plutons to the south. On the right-hand shore lies the granite — precipitous pink cliffs with pine trees clinging to tiny crevices of soil on the surface. On the left-hand shoreline lies the quartzite — brilliant white hills interspersed with steep-sided, boulder-strewn valleys and decorated with twisted ribbons of dark volcanic rock. On a misty morning, or in the dazzling late-afternoon sun, the scene is unbelievably beautiful! Continue for 2.5 km to the eastern end of George Lake **B**, where a wooden dock serves as the take-out for the short portage to Freeland Lake. The portage bypasses an old logging dam, once used to control water levels and timber flow between the two lakes.

2nd Segment: Freeland Lake to the La Cloche Silhouette Trail (2 km paddle)

Freeland Lake is shallow and its shoreline flatter and less dramatic than that of George Lake. But Freeland is one of Killarney's few "live" lakes, less severely affected by acid rain than many in the park and home to more abundant marine plant and animal life. Beaver lodges, and often beavers themselves, can be seen along the shore. Weeds and water lilies wrap themselves around the paddle, and the waterway resembles a slalom course at times as it weaves among floating mats of vegetation. Toward its eastern end the lake becomes increasingly overgrown, and the approach to the take-out at the Sealey's Lake portage can be awkwardly marshy if water levels are low. Old portage signs that are still visible on trees on the southeast shore may confuse paddlers as to the take-out location, tempting one to land too soon. Ignore them, and continue to the very end of Freeland Lake and up the narrows into Kakakise Creek. The take-out C, marked by a yellow portage sign, is on the right-hand side of the channel where the trees converge toward the creek. Leave your boat pulled ashore here and continue on foot.

3rd Segment: La Cloche Silhouette Trail to "The Crack" (3.5 km hike)

Follow the portage path for 100 m up the hill to Sealey's Lake and turn left onto the La Cloche Silhouette Trail. The trail is gentle and easy to follow for the first 2 km as it travels eastward through a wooded lowland. At Kakakise Lake it cuts across an old beaver dam D, where the footing is not always reliable, and then hugs the shoreline around the lake's northwestern corner. Here it crosses an impossible-looking boulder-strewn path that

View from Killarney Ridge above "The Crack"

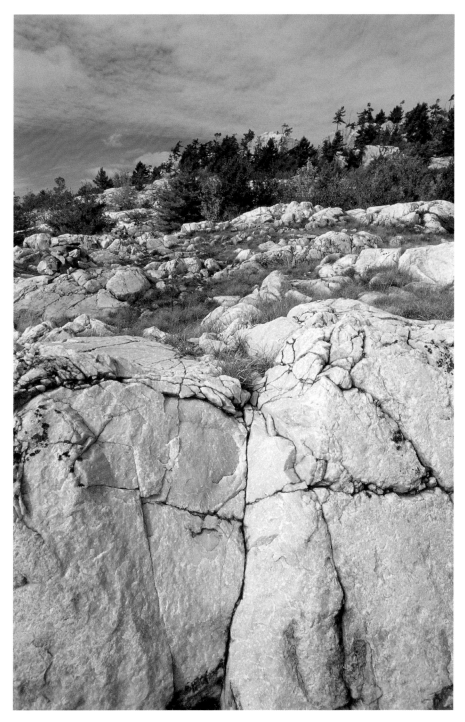

Approach to "The Crack"over quartzite ridges

heads almost vertically up the hill to the left — the perilous portage over the mountain ridge to Killarney Lake 1440 m away! About 200 m past this portage the trail crosses a small creek, then turns sharply left and climbs steeply away from Kakakise Lake. After a short scramble through the trees it emerges onto a ridge. For the next kilometre the trail alternates between exposed quartzite ridges and small, forested glens. Cairns mark the route across the ridges, but it's easy to lose the trail in all the sparkling white rock. Aim for the left-hand side of the topmost ridge where a large gash in the rock will become visible — "The Crack". The trail makes its way through the cleft, clambering upward over enormous boulders between vertical cliff walls for the final 100 m to the summit. The view from the top is glorious! Killarney and OSA lakes lie below, and behind them the quartzite ridges of the La Cloche Mountains stretch skyward — the Blue Ridge to the right and the Killarney Ridge to the left. This makes an ideal picnic place and a needed rest stop.

4th Segment: Homeward (3.5 km hike, 5.5 km paddle, 50 m portage)

The homeward journey retraces the outward route, presumably with less huffing and puffing on the descent. After crossing Kakakise Creek D, watch for the right-hand turn, where the trail leaves the wider track. And back at Freeland and George lakes, be ready for a strenuous paddle. Typically the afternoon wind is an enthusiastic westerly, funnelled between the ridges into the face of the paddler. The channel at the western end of George Lake will be a welcome sight at the end of a long and exhilarating day!

Bell Lake and Silver Peak

This excursion ascends Killarney's loftiest summit, Silver Peak, to take in the magnificent view over the park and beyond — on a clear day, more than 50 km in all directions! The climb is a strenuous 318 m from lake level to summit, and the approach involves 3 km of paddling and 5 km of hiking, so the excursion is an invigorating full-day's outing. Although the paddling portion can be limited to an easy linear route with no portages — a means of simply getting to and from the hiking trail — it is much more satisfying to extend it over a series of short portages into a loop through Log Boom and Johnnie lakes.

• Main Route: 10 km hike, 6.5–7.5 km paddle, 0–350 m portage(s)

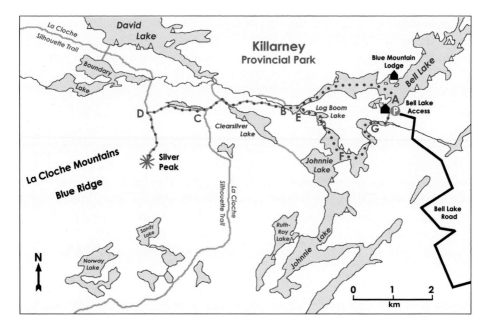

Access

- From the park office return 20 km east along Hwy 637, turn left onto the Bell Lake Road and follow it for 9 km to the Bell Lake Access parking area and boat launch. Note that during the summer months you may also pick up a permit at the Bell Lake Access, provided that reservations have been made in advance.

Route Description

1st Segment: Bell Lake (3.2 km paddle)

From the Bell Lake launch **A** paddle north, keeping to the left-hand shore, and follow the shoreline as it curves into the lake's western arm opposite Blue Mountain Lodge. Where the arm narrows about halfway down, Silver Peak comes into view, its massive white summit rising impressively out of the surrounding forest. Continue to the far western end of the lake and pull your kayak or canoe ashore at the small clearing **B** to the left of the creek.

2nd Segment: Bell Lake to Silver Peak (5 km hike)

From Bell Lake follow the hiking trail inland for 1.5 km to the head of Clearsilver Lake. Here it jogs right for 200 m along the portage to David Lake, then left for 300 m up a rocky slope to meet the La Cloche Silhouette Trail **C**. Turn right and continue westward for another 1.5 km to the Silver Peak access trail **D**, which exits on the left. Over this entire distance, the route travels through a hardwood forest of maple and birch.

Underfoot the terrain is gentle, with only occasional muddy or rocky sections, and the trail is wide and easy to follow.

The character of the landscape changes dramatically during the ascent to Silver Peak. The access trail climbs with breathtaking steepness, rising almost 300 m in just over 1 km. The footing becomes increasingly rough on the way up, scrambling across loose rocks and exposed roots along the edge of a pretty stream, then slithering over smooth quartzite outcroppings at higher elevations. The vegetation becomes sparse, the hardwood forests giving way to scattered oaks and pines, and eventually to bald rock fringed with grasses and shrubs. Toward the summit the trail swings to the right and levels out slightly through a wooded glen, giving a welcome break before the final short push to the top.

Silver Peak, at 362 m above the level of Georgian Bay, is the highest point in the Killarney landscape, and the view from the summit is appropriately stunning. To the south, small lakes dot the foreground and Georgian Bay sparkles in the distance. To the west lie the shimmering ridges of the La Cloche Mountains with Killarney Lake nestled between them and the silhouette of Manitoulin Island in the background. And to the north and east the vast wilderness of "Rainbow Country" stretches away to the horizon, interrupted only by the smokestacks of Sudbury. This outlook made an excellent location for a fire tower in the early 1900s; its remnants can still be seen on the rocks at the summit. Today it makes a perfect setting for a restorative picnic lunch before you set out on the return journey.

Approach to Silver Peak from Bell Lake

143

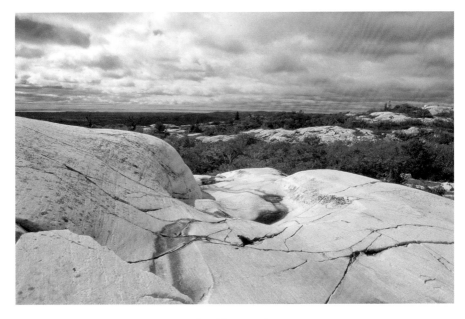

Smooth quartzite outcroppings at the Silver Peak summit

3rd Segment: Homeward via Log Boom & Johnnie Lakes (5 km hike, 3—4 km paddle, 0—350 m portage(s)

From the summit retrace the outward route along the trail to your boat B. For a simple, speedy return, paddle back along Bell Lake to the launch A via the outward route. Or, for pleasant variety and added challenge, the return route can be extended into a loop. Paddle 300 m across the western arm of Bell Lake and take the portage leading to Log Boom Lake E. This is the first of three very short (5–10 m) easy portages around unnavigable sections of a small stream that flows south from Bell Lake through Log Boom Lake and into Johnnie Lake — a total distance of only 1 km. As Log Boom Lake's name suggests, the stream was once a logging waterway, where inland timber was marshalled and driven on the spring surge to the Mahzenazing River and along to the sawmill at Collins Inlet.

Settling back into your boat after all the ins and outs along the stream, follow the left-hand shoreline of Johnnie Lake southward for 1 km. At the narrows F where the shoreline swings east, take a final look back at Silver Peak looming against the horizon. Then turn left through the narrows and follow the winding course of the lake north and east. There are several backcountry campsites along the shore, and some eye-catching outcrops of brilliant white rock. About 2 km past the narrows, a 5 m portage (to the left) is necessary to bypass a beaver dam G, and on the left-hand shore just

200 m beyond the dam is the take-out for the 300 m portage up the hill to the Bell Lake parking lot—this final trudge bringing to an end a most satisfying day's journey.

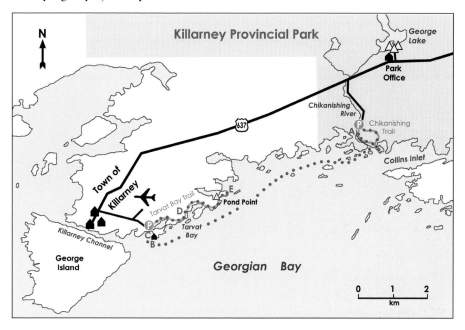

Chikanishing River and Georgian Bay Coast

This excursion leaves the quartzite hills of Killarney's interior and makes its way along the rugged, windswept granite of Killarney's Georgian Bay shore. It combines a coastal paddle from the Chikanishing River to the Red Rock Lighthouse with two short hikes – the Chikanishing Trail at the eastern end of the paddle and the Tarvat Bay Trail at the western end. The paddling portion of the route, 7 km each way, must be undertaken with great circumspection, as wind and waves along the exposed coastline can be hazardous. If paddling conditions are prohibitive, the two hiking trails can be undertaken independently, both being easily accessible by car from Hwy 637.

• Main Route: 6.5–10.5 km hike, 14 km paddle
• Alternative: 6.5–10.5 km hike

Access

• From the park office continue west on Hwy 637 for 1.5 km and turn left to the Chickanishing Access Point parking area and boat launch.

Georgian Bay shoreline at the mouth of the Chikanishing River

Route Description
1st Segment: Chikanishing Trail (3.5 km hike)

From the parking area the Chikanishing Trail follows its namesake river downstream to Georgian Bay, then makes its way eastward along the shore to a rocky point before looping inland to return to the trailhead. Interpretive boxes along the trail contain information about the area's natural features and human history.

The coastal rocks overlook the western entrance to Collins Inlet, a narrow passage that runs eastward along a geological fault for 20 km to Beaverstone Bay near the mouth of the French River. It was once a major transportation route, a sheltered corridor for travellers crossing the top of Georgian Bay. Native paddlers used it in ancient times. Voyageurs used it during the fur trade years of the eighteenth and nineteenth centuries, carrying trade goods westward to the major posts on Lake Superior and beaver pelts eastward for shipment to Europe. Loggers followed in the late 1800s and the early decades of the 1900s, gathering timber from inland rivers into huge booms, which they towed down the channel to the now-abandoned mill town of Collins Inlet at the mouth of the Mahzenazing River. Some historical artifacts remain, like the iron rings visible from the Chikanishing Trail, once used to tether the log booms. But Collins Inlet is a quieter waterway today, its usual visitors being canoes, kayaks and other recreational craft.

2nd Segment: Chikanishing River to Red Rock Lighthouse (7 km paddle)

Back at the parking area, launch your kayak or canoe into the Chikanishing River **A** and paddle downstream for 200 m along its winding course between granite cliffs on the left and marshland on the right. At the river mouth turn right and paddle into Georgian Bay. The route to the Red Rock Lighthouse, 7 km along the shoreline to the west-southwest, is littered with small islands and rocky shoals. Frequent consultation with a good map is essential for safe and accurate navigation; pay close attention to landmarks for the return journey. The beauty of the coast — its red granite rocks dappled with multicoloured lichens and topped with twisted pines — makes it well worth the effort of finding the way along it!

The Red Rock Lighthouse **B** is an obvious landmark at the western end of the paddle. Like most Great Lakes lighthouses, it was automated in the early 1980s and now serves as an unmanned navigation beacon. But its history stretches back to 1867, when it was established to guide boats through the shoals and channels to the village of Killarney. For more than a century it was maintained by lighthouse keepers, who lived in the small house behind the tower. Curve to the right around the lighthouse peninsula and aim for the small boulder-beach amid the red granite bordering the bay. Turn sharply right just before reaching the shore; a tiny inlet will be visible sheltered behind a long finger of rock. At the head of the inlet is a 5 m strip of sand **C** where you may leave your boat during the hike that follows.

3rd Segment: Tarvat Bay Trail (3–7 km hike)

Over the embankment behind the beach is a gravel track that leads to the lighthouse. Turn left onto the track, away from the lighthouse, walk past the metal gate and then turn right almost immediately at the small parking area that marks the start of the Tarvat Bay Trail. The trail lies on land belonging to the village of Killarney, whose residents undertake its maintenance. It is marked with yellow plastic blazes and flagging on trees through wooded areas, and yellow painted arrows and cairns over sections of open rock. It winds along the edge of Lighthouse Lake, crosses a marshy area at its eastern end, then

Red Rock Lighthouse

Tar vat on the Georgian Bay shore

clambers over a rocky headland and along the shore to Tarvat Bay. Here, on the shore just to the right of the trail, can be found the apparatus that gives the bay its name D. In the heyday of Killarney's fishery in the 1800s, fishermen brought their cotton nets to the bay, where they dipped them into heated vats filled with protective tar and spread them to dry over the surrounding rocks. The smell of tar permeates the place to this day, but the Killarney fishery is largely gone, the fish stocks depleted by overfishing and by invaders like the sea lamprey, and the fish-spawning beds choked with debris from the logging industry.

The weary may wish to turn back here. But for anyone with energy to spare, the trail continues beyond Tarvat Bay, curving inland through a wooded area before returning to the coast. It then follows the rocky shoreline eastward for another kilometre, crossing a red shingle beach, cutting over Pond Point, passing a primitive campsite nestled in a tiny bay and ending at a rocky promontory E with a splendid view toward the La Cloche Mountains. The trail markers over this latter section are sporadic at best, but their absence should not present a problem, as the route simply follows the water's edge.

4th Segment: Homeward (3–7 km hike, 7 km paddle)

Turning back, either from Tarvat Bay D or from one of the points further along the trail, retrace the outward route to your boat C. The wind may have arisen for the afternoon paddle back along the shore to the Chikanishing River, but as the typical wind is westerly it should at least be blowing with you.

Alternative: Omit the Paddle (10.5 km hike)

If wind and wave conditions prevent the exposed coastal paddle, the two hikes can be accessed by road from Hwy 637 instead. To reach the Tarvat Bay Trailhead, drive into Killarney and turn left onto Ontario Street (following the Killarney Airport sign). After 1.2 km take the right-hand fork and follow the rough track leading to the Red Rock Lighthouse. Just before the gate, pull into the small parking area to the left of the track and continue on foot from there.

Other Paddling & Hiking Opportunities

Killarney Park boasts some of the finest hiking and paddling opportunities in the province. The excursions in this chapter visit several of the highlights, but many others are possible and other excellent guidebooks have been written about them. Armed with the park map and some imagination, it is possible to invent your own routes, and spend many delightful holidays in and around the park.

Paddling
There are dozens of paddling possibilities on the park's inland lakes, with lengths ranging from a relaxing weekend outing to week-long adventures of arduous proportions including long and strenuous portages over significant ridges of land. The alternative, for those allergic to portages, is an exploration of the Georgian Bay or Collins Inlet shorelines, although these are exposed waterways that require solid paddling and navigational skills to undertake them with safety.

Hiking
- The Granite Ridge Trail is a 2 km loop that follows a ridge on the south side of the park, with pleasant views over Georgian Bay to the south and the La Cloche Mountains to the north. Access is on the south side of Hwy 637 opposite the George Lake campground entrance. A trail guide is available from the Park Office.
- The Cranberry Bog Trail is a 4 km loop that explores the granite formation on the south side of George Lake and visits several wetlands. Access is from the George Lake campground near site #103, and a trail guide is available from the park office.
- The George Island Trail is a 7.5 km loop through an interesting variety of habitats found on George Island. The trailhead is across the channel from the Sportsman's Inn in Killarney, and the inn provides ferry service to the island for a nominal fee.
- The La Cloche Silhouette Trail is a 100 km loop that traverses the La Cloche Mountain ridges and valleys in between. The entire trail may be undertaken as a backpacking trip, normally taking 7–10 days. Smaller sections of it may be hiked as day-trips, starting from the George Lake campground or accessing the trail from other locations by boat.

Chikanishing River

Practical Information

Killarney Provincial Park

- Park Season: open year-round.
- Park Permit: required for all Killarney Park users. Permits are available from the park office at the entrance to the George Lake campground.
- Camping: Killarney's drive-in campground has 126 sites on the shore of George Lake, with toilets and a comfort station. These sites are popular, and should be reserved well in advance for the summer months and holiday weekends. Killarney also has 178 interior campsites scattered on the shorelines of its lakes and along its backpacking trail. Backcountry routes must be registered and campsites reserved at the park office. During the summer it is also possible (and advisable) to book interior sites in advance. In July and August, you may obtain your permit at the Bell Lake Access Point if you have made a reservation ahead of time.
- A can and bottle ban is in effect in Killarney Park's interior, which includes all lakes and day-use trails as well as interior campsites.
- Information: park office (705) 287-2900, Ontario Parks Reservation Service 1-888-668-7275, www.ontarioparks.com.

- The Friends of Killarney Park is a non-profit association established in 1986 to help park staff provide educational program and publications that encourage public appreciation of Killarney's natural environment. For information contact the Friends at (705) 287-2800, www.friendsofkillarneypark.ca.

Maps & Publications

- The Friends of Killarney Park have published an excellent 1:50,000 topographic map showing the park's hiking trails, portages and interior campsites, and indicating elevations and points of interest in the area. The reverse side of the map gives a description of the natural features and human history of the park, a guide for hiking and paddling in the park, and a summary of park regulations. This map is a must for travelling in the park, and can be purchased at the park's George Lake and Bell Lake offices and from outdoor stores across the province.
- The Friends also publish a canoe guide and several park trail guides, available at the George Lake and Bell Lake offices.

Supplies, Accommodations & Attractions Outside the Park

- Basic supplies, accommodations and overflow camping are available in the town of Killarney, 10 km past the main park entrance at the western terminus of Hwy 637. Killarney, has a long and interesting history as a Great Lakes port, supply post and fishing community. For more information see www.killarneyhistory.com.
- Boat rentals and outfitting services are available locally from Killarney Mountain Lodge & Outfitters, 6.5 km west of the George Lake entrance on Hwy 637, 1-800-461-1117, www.killarney.com, and from Killarney Kanoes in Sudbury at 1-888-461-4446, www.killarneykanoes.com.
- The Sportsman's Inn, one of several providers of accommodation in the town of Killarney, has some excellent general local information on its website, www.sportsmansinn.ca.

- Blue Mountain Lodge provides accommodation on Bell Lake, giving easy access to Silver Peak and the eastern side of the park. For information contact the lodge at (705) 287-2197.

Georgian Bay shoreline along the Tar Bay Trail

Acid Rain in Killarney

Acid rain is a type of atmospheric pollution. It forms when acidic compounds become airborne, travel on wind currents and join with water molecules that fall to earth as rain or snow.

The two most common acidic compounds are sulphur dioxide and nitrous oxide. Sulphur dioxide is a waste product from industrial metal smelting, oil refining, gas processing and coal-fired electrical generation. Nitrous oxide is emitted during the burning of fossil fuels, the largest sources being motor vehicles and heating systems. Sulphur dioxide and nitrous oxide combine in the air with water vapour to produce sulphuric acid and nitric acid, both highly corrosive agents.

Acidity is measured on the pH scale, which ranges from 0 (extremely acidic) to 14 (extremely alkaline). The pH scale is logarithmic, with each unit representing a ten-fold increase or decrease in acidity from the next unit. Distilled water is neutral, with a pH of 7. At the alkaline end of the scale, oven and liquid drain cleaners have a pH of 13 to 14. At the acidic end, vinegar has a pH of 2, human stomach acid a pH of 1 and car battery acid a pH of 0. The pH of healthy lakewater is between 6 and 8.

Pollution by acid rain affects aquatic ecosystems by increasing the acidity (decreasing the pH) of lakewater so that it is unable to support the natural numbers of organisms and diversity of species. Freshwater clams, shrimps and insect larvae begin to die when the pH drops below 6. The eggs of most species of fish and amphibians fail to hatch at a pH less than 5, and below 4.5 the water is considered sterile, unable to support any aquatic life. Lakes located in naturally acidic environments — where the surrounding rocks, soil and vegetation are composed of acidic substances like quartzite and peat — are more susceptible to the effects of acid rain than are alkaline environments rich in limestone and deep in soil. Acids also react with metals like aluminum and mercury, releasing them from the soil and leaching them into the water system where they can accumulate in poisonous quantities in the organisms living there. As species lower in the food chain succumb to the acids and toxic metals, species higher up the chain die out from the loss of their natural food sources, even if they are not directly affected by the acids and metals themselves.

Killarney's lakes suffered severely in the 1960s and 1970s from acid rain generated by the nearby smelters in Sudbury and by industrial activities further afield. The natural acidity of the quartzite bedrock and the thinness of the soil reduced the ability of the environment to buffer the effects of acid rain. Measurements taken in Lumsden Lake, for example, showed a drop in pH from 6.8 in 1961 to only 4.4 in 1971, representing more than a thousand-fold increase in acidity during the decade. Entire aquatic ecosystems suffered from the altered water chemistry, and whole species vanished from the park. Being so highly vulnerable, Killarney's lakes were among the first in North America to succumb, and therefore among the first to be studied. Data collected in Killarney helped in the formulation of strict new environmental controls to reduce industrial sulphur and other toxic emissions across the continent.

Forty years of study at Killarney have seen first the collapse and then the gradual recovery of the park's lakes. The Sudbury-based Cooperative Freshwater Ecology Unit, composed of government, environmental and industrial scientists, conducts samplings of the water and surveys the lakes' populations every summer. In 2001, for the first time in three decades, young wild lake trout were captured in George Lake — an encouraging reminder of nature's resilience in the face of human interference!

Chapter 11

Mississagi

Overview

Mississagi Provincial Park is located 60 km inland from the North Channel of Lake Huron. It is a large, natural-environment park set among the rolling Algoma hills. Not on the road to anywhere else, 25 km from the nearest community of Elliot Lake, and more than a six-hour drive from the population centres of southern Ontario, Mississagi is not well known and is easily overlooked. The traveller who makes the detour, however, is rewarded with many opportunities for paddling and hiking, and miles of peace and solitude.

Outcroppings of hard, shiny rock in beautiful shades of pink and white are frequently seen along the park trails. This is the ancient bedrock of the Mississagi area — quartzite. It formed more than 2 billion years ago when a bubble of quartz-rich magma solidified deep in the Earth's crust along the boundary between the Superior and Southern geological provinces. Subsequent movements in the crust compressed and reshaped the rock, metamorphosing it into quartzite. Dense and erosion-resistant, it withstood the more recent scouring of glaciers, which removed the overlying softer rock and left the quartzite exposed, most prominently at the tops of hills like Old Baldy and the cliff overlooking the Brush Lakes. The following excursions visit these two geologically interesting hilltops, but it is easy to be distracted from the geology underfoot because the views above are so magnificent!

Access
- Take Hwy 17 west from Sudbury 160 km or east from Sault Ste. Marie 190 km.
- Exit onto Hwy 108 north and drive 25 km to Elliot Lake, where the road changes to Hwy 639.
- Continue along Hwy 639 for another 25 km to the Mississagi Park entrance on the right.
- Proceed to the access point listed at the start of each excursion.

McKenzie Trail lookout over the Brush Lakes

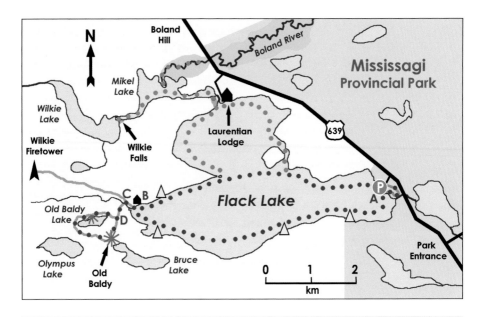

Flack Lake and Old Baldy

The route described here is not long or strenuous, with just 12 km of paddling and two short hiking loops totalling less than 6 km, although one of these loops includes a 215 m climb to the summit of Old Baldy. The paddling portion can be extended by portaging from the north end of Flack Lake into Mikel Lake to explore part of the Boland River system.

- Main Route: 5.7 km hike, 12 km paddle
- Alternative(s): 5.7 km hike, 18+ km paddle, 260 m portage(s)

Access
- Continue 1.5 km past the main entrance to Mississagi Park, turn left to the Flack Lake boat launch and parking area, and buy a permit from the self-serve station.

Route Description
1st Segment: Flack Lake Nature Trail (0.7 km hike)
Beginning and ending at the launch area **A**, the Flack Lake Nature Trail loops around the mouth of a small creek. Along the way, it crosses an impressive bed of ripple-rock. Formed by wave action on the shore of an ancient beach, the original ridges of sand were buried by subsequent layers and compressed deep beneath the surface to form rock. Many millennia later, glaciers removed these covering layers and exposed the ripples,

appropriately, near the shore of a modern-day lake. The trail also passes the rotting and rusting remnants of a logging camp, a reminder of the park's human history. Logging continues in the area outside the park today, as the swaths of barren hillside and the bulging logging trucks attest.

2nd Segment: Flack Lake Launch to Take-out (6 km paddle)

Paddle from the launch **A** along the south shore of Flack Lake. The shoreline here is rugged, with tangles of dense bush growing right down to the water's edge, and jumbles of jagged rock rising up from the depths to meet it. There are several primitive campsites along the shore, but otherwise no sign of human habitation until the western end of the lake. Here sits an abandoned cabin **B**, which was once used by the keepers of the (now also abandoned) Wilkie Fire Tower. Pull your canoe or kayak ashore and leave it here while you hike up Old Baldy.

3rd Segment: Old Baldy Loop (5 km hike)

Follow the track leading inland from the cabin for 0.2 km. Turn left at the signpost to Old Baldy **C**, and begin the climb. Soon after crossing a small stream 0.5 km up the hill **D**, turn sharply right onto a less-well-travelled

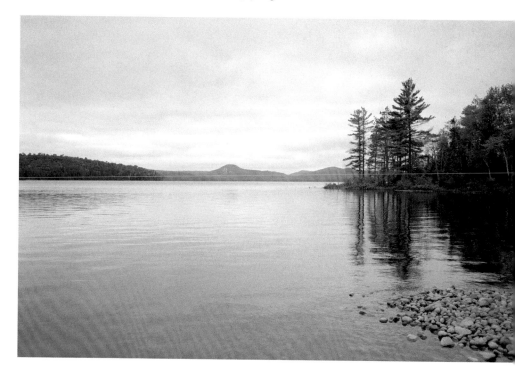

Looking across Flack Lake toward Old Baldy

View from the summit of Old Baldy

path. It skirts the smooth, rocky north shore of Old Baldy Lake, and then crosses a boggy patch at the western end where the trail can be somewhat elusive. Turning southeast from the bog, the trail climbs steeply to the summit. The view on a clear day is glorious. In the foreground to the south are Bruce and Olympus lakes. To the west, poking through a thick blanket of forest, is the Wilkie Fire Tower. To the east lies Flack Lake and a bird's-eye view of the route just paddled. And to the north, past Laurentian Lodge at the north end of Flack Lake, Hwy 639 can be seen climbing up the considerable slope of Boland Hill. And underfoot, of course, is the brilliant white quartzite mentioned earlier. The summit makes an excellent spot to enjoy a picnic lunch before descending along the well-worn path on the eastern side of Old Baldy, which rejoins the trail back to the cabin **B**.

4th Segment: Homeward (6 km paddle)
Return via the same route along the southern shore of Flack Lake, or for variation follow the northern shoreline.

Alternative: Extend the Paddle (5.7 km hike, 18+ km paddle, 260 m portage)

The homeward paddle can be extended by paddling to the north end of Flack Lake and taking the 130 m portage (which skirts a pretty waterfall and a cluster of cottages at Laurentian Lodge) into Mikel Lake. The Boland River passes through Mikel Lake, and if water levels are sufficiently high, it is possible to paddle upstream along its meandering course through the marshlands, or downstream to Wilkie Falls and beyond.

Semiwite–Helenbar Lakes and McKenzie Trail

This route has many variations for both paddling and hiking. The paddle can be just a quick way to get to the trail for a long hike to the Stag Lake Peatland lookout. Or you can extend the paddle to explore Semiwite and Helenbar lakes, with a short leg-stretch on the trail to the Brush Lakes Lookout. An energetic traveller who starts early can even do both the long paddle and the long hike. In any case, the excursion undoubtedly deserves a full day.

• Main Route: 4 km hike, 7 km paddle, 980 m portage(s)
• Alternative(s): 12 km hike, 15 km paddle, 980 m portage(s)

Access

• Turn right at the main entrance to the park, buy a permit from the park office, and leave the car at the day-use parking area and boat launch on Semiwite Lake.

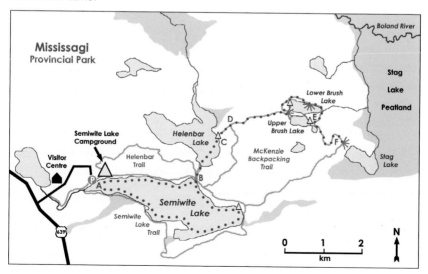

Stag Lake Peatland

Route Description
1st Segment: Semiwite Lake (2.5 to 6 km paddle, 490 m portage)
From the launch A paddle east to the portage into Helenbar Lake B. The direct (2.5 km) route along the north shore of Semiwite Lake passes beside the campground. The longer (6 km), more scenic route follows the shoreline in a counter-clockwise direction. Along the south shore the terrain is rugged, with steep cliffs and several small marshlands. The eastern and northern shorelines are gentler, with gravel banks and sandy beaches. The portage into Helenbar Lake is not difficult.

2nd Segment: Helenbar Lake (0.5 to 6 km paddle)
From the portage, the direct route is just 0.5 km to the campsite on the eastern shore of Helenbar Lake C, where your boat can be left during the hike that follows. For a longer paddle (up to 6 km), allow yourself to be tempted by the arms of the lake stretching between the hills to the north and west.

Helenbar Lake is the site of an extraordinary tidbit of human history. In late June of 1946 a young RCAF pilot, 25-year-old Bill McKenzie, was flying a high-speed state-of-the-art military plane, a Gloster Meteor, over northern Ontario en route to an air show in Hamilton. Equipment difficulties and poor weather sent him off course, and he eventually ran out of fuel and had to ditch the plane — in Helenbar Lake. McKenzie managed to swim away from the wreckage, but was unable to salvage any gear. Remarkably, he survived on the southeastern shore of Helenbar Lake for 26 days, with only a few wild berries for food, before being rescued by a fishing party from Laurentian Lodge. The plane was later retrieved from the lake, but a few relics still remain scattered along the shore — incongruous bits of metal in the Mississagi wilderness. The park's backpacking trail bears McKenzie's name.

3rd Segment: McKenzie Backpacking Trail to Brush Lakes Lookout (2 km hike)

From the campsite C, follow the woodland trail leading upward and inland 0.5 km to the junction D with the McKenzie Backpacking Trail. Turn left, and continue 1.5 km along the trail. The character of the forest changes as the trail climbs, the lush vegetation of the lowland giving way to scattered pines and oaks in the harsher conditions of the highland. The trail finally opens onto a superb cliff-top lookout eastward, with the two small Brush Lakes in the foreground and the Stag Lake Peatland between the hills in the distance. The beautiful white and pink rock underfoot is quartzite. This is an excellent spot to rest or have a picnic, before either turning back to your boat or continuing on the trail to the Stag Lake Peatland lookout.

4th Segment: Brush Lakes Lookout to Stag Lake Peatland Lookout (4 km hike)

The trail descends with alarming steepness from the lookout to the edge of Lower Brush Lake 125 m below. It then follows the shoreline, with many fine views back across the lake, and crosses the thin finger of land E that separates Lower from Upper Brush Lake. The trail continues southeastward over rough terrain and arrives at a lookout F above the magnificent Stag Lake Peatland.

After your walk through so much leafy forest, the peatland comes as a surprise — an expanse of barren, boreal bog in the midst of the woodland, and a reminder that Mississagi Park lies in the transition zone between southern and northern climates. Peat is an accumulation of organic matter. It forms in conditions of low oxygen that prevent normal decomposition, so that plant debris is deposited at a rate faster than it can be broken down. Such conditions are met in the Stag Lake Peatland, where the surrounding terrain prevents good drainage, a meandering stream keeps the soil saturated and stagnant, and the cool northern climate keeps evaporation to a minimum. Soil chemistry in a peatland is typically acidic and nutrient-poor. Only the few hardy species that have specially adapted to it can survive here — a few shrubs like Labrador Tea and alder, a collection of grasses, mats of sphagnum moss, and the occasional straggly black spruce tree.

5th Segment: Homeward (2–6 km hike, depending on turn-around point, 3.5 km paddle, 490 m portage)

Return via the same route and enjoy the scenery from a different perspective.

Other Paddling & Hiking Opportunities

Paddling

For paddling, there are many opportunities, from easy, day-long meanders around the park's more accessible lakes, to gruelling multi-day expeditions in remote areas with long, rough portages and white-water river paddling.

Hiking

Mississagi has six hiking trails, ranging from the 0.7 km Flack Lake Nature Trail to the 22 km McKenzie Backpacking Trail. Three of the other trails begin at the Semiwite Lake campground: the Semiwite Creek Trail (1.2 km), the Helenbar Lake Lookout Trail (7 km) and the Semiwite Lake Trail (12 km). The one remaining trail, and also perhaps the most lovely and varied, is the Cobre Lake Trail (11 km), about 10 km north of the campground entrance.

Practical Information

Mississagi Provincial Park:

- Park Season: open from mid-May to mid-October.
- Park Permit: required for all users of Mississagi Park, available from the park office or at the self-serve kiosk at the Flack Lake launch.
- Camping: Mississagi has 94 campsites and some basic facilities in its campground on the north shore of Semiwite Lake. There are also several primitive paddle-in campsites along the shorelines of Flack, Semiwite and Helenbar lakes and two hike-in sites on the Brush Lakes. Note that the park is not on the Ontario Parks reservation service, but availability is not generally a problem.
- The Visitor Centre carries some basic camping supplies, souvenirs and publications, and staff are available to give information about the park.
- Information: park office (705) 848-2806 (May–October) or (705) 865-2021 (off-season), www.ontarioparks.com.

Maps & Publications:

- Chrismar Mapping Services has published, as part of its Adventure Map series, an excellent, waterproof, 1:50,000 topographic map of the Mississagi area, complete with hiking trails, portages, campsites and many points of interest. It is available from the park's Visitor Centre and from many outdoor stores across the province. It is a must for hiking and paddling in the park.
- Mississagi Park has an excellent hiking trails pamphlet, available from the park office or visitor centre.

Supplies, Accommodations & Attractions Outside the Park:

- Laurentian Lodge, on the north shore of Flack Lake, just outside the park boundary, has roofed accommodation and serviced campsites. Contact the lodge at (705) 848-0423, www.laurentianlodge.com.
- Elliot Lake, 25 km to the south of the park, has more extensive supplies and accommodations. The town developed around the uranium mining industry, which was active in the area from 1952 to the mid-1990s, when the last mine closed. Many of the former mine sites, just south of Mississagi Park, are now undergoing reclamation to return them to their natural condition. Contact the Elliot Lake tourism office at 1-800-661-6192, www.cityofelliotlake.com or www.elliotlake.com.
- The Voyageur Trail: On the way to Mississagi Park, 6.2 km north along Hwy 108 from Hwy 17, an unobtrusive marker on the west side of the road indicates the start of a hiking trail. This is the magnificent Voyageur Trail, which traverses some of the most rugged, remote and beautiful landscape in Ontario. Begun in 1975, it is envisaged to stretch some 1100 kilometres along the North Channel of Lake Huron and the northern shore of Lake Superior, all the way from Manitoulin Island in the east to Thunder Bay in the west. Roughly half that distance, in discontinuous sections of trail, has been completed to date. The 23.5 km Coureur de Bois section south of Elliot Lake is the eastern extremity of the present trail. For information contact the Voyageur Trail Association at 1-877-393-4003, www3.sympatico.ca/voyageur.trail.

Chapter 12

A Taste of Superior

Overview

Lake Superior, the "inland sea" whose immense size and savage moods have inspired generations of adventurers, artists and songwriters, is the final stop in this collection of excursions. But anyone who ventures along Superior's northern shore will surely return—its spectacular landscape, its treacherous waters and its uncompromising character will draw the traveller back time and time again.

Lake Superior is the largest lake (by surface area) in the world, measuring 650 km in an arc from end to end, 260 km at its widest, and 405 m deep. It contains 10% of the Earth's fresh water supply — enough to cover North and South America to a depth of one foot. It is such an enormous body of water that its temperature remains nearly constant, averaging a chilly 8°C, though sheltered shallow bays can become almost comfortable toward the end of summer. It moderates the climate of the surrounding land, tempering the harshness of winter and the heat of summer. And it creates its own weather systems, producing thick fog-banks, fierce winds and towering waves rivalling those of the oceans. It is an unforgiving environment, known for its unpredictability, and anyone who ventures out upon it must be mindful of its power.

Lake Superior's shoreline landscape is magnificently rugged—wave-battered rocks and storm-tossed logs, beaches of fine white sand or enormous rounded cobbles, rivers plunging wildly down steep-walled valleys out of the interior highlands, tangles of stunted spruce, stands of white birch, rocks encrusted with lichens, hollows carpeted with moss, marshy lakes and expansive bogs—kilometre after kilometre of remote boreal wilderness.

The underlying rock is part of the ancient Superior Province of the Canadian Shield, formed 3 to 2.5 billion years ago from eroded sediments and volcanic material, and metamorphosed by subsequent geologic events. About 1 billion years ago a shift in the Earth's crust tore a massive, crescent-shaped gash in the North American continent — the 2000 km Midcontinental Rift. Part of this rift eventually filled with water and became Lake Superior. The subterranean turbulence that caused the rift also spawned a network of smaller fractures. Along some of these fractures,

Beach overlooking Devil's Chair

planes of rock slipped away, creating dramatic cliffs and impressive piles of talus (rock debris at the base of a cliff). Molten material oozed through other fractures, erupted, and then solidified to form volcanic rock, often pockmarked with gas bubbles and crystal deposits. With the passing of glaciers and their meltwaters in more recent times, the softer volcanic rock became sculpted into peculiar shapes or eroded completely away, leaving caves and passageways behind.

For Native Ojibwe travellers, dramatic geology has always been intimately connected with their spiritual world. In places where the natural elements of earth, air and water meet — where a cliff face plunges into a deep lake or a cave opens into a hillside, for instance — the realms of humans and manitous converge. Such places are common along the Superior shoreline, and so the shore is amply populated with spirits. It is home to Nanabosho, the delightfully impetuous and much loved manitou who is protector of the Ojibwe people. And the lake is also home to Mishepeshu, the great horned lynx who lurks in the underwater kingdom and controls the wind and waves with an irritable flick of his tail. Native paddlers left offerings of appeasement at sacred sites along the shore and painted red-ochre images on waterside cliffs to honour the manitous. The voyageurs who followed, hauling beaver pelts and trade goods back and forth along Superior's north shore during the seventeenth and eighteenth centuries, and even the tourists who ply the waters today, continue prudently to leave offerings at these sites, for on this wonderful shore the distinction between legend and reality can become hazy indeed!

Examples of these natural features and human imprints can be found within Lake Superior Provincial Park, a vast (1556 km^2) swath of wilderness on Superior's northeastern shore. The park was established in 1944 to protect the area's unique natural environment, but it received little attention and few visitors until Hwy 17 finally broke through the impenetrable terrain and was officially opened in 1960. Since then the park has become increasingly popular, and its facilities have come to include three camp-grounds, several day-use picnic areas, eight backcountry paddling routes, ten hiking trails and the splendid 65 km coastal backpacking trail.

The excursions in this chapter, scattered along the coastline of Lake Superior Provincial Park, give just a taste of the beauty of Lake Superior's landscape. As in previous chapters, each excursion includes both a hiking and a paddling segment. The paddling segments, however, should be undertaken only by people with solid paddling skills and always with great circumspection, being mindful of the lake's moods. If in doubt, you may omit the paddling segment, as most of the excursions are also designed to be tackled entirely by land. The Friends of Lake Superior Provincial Park

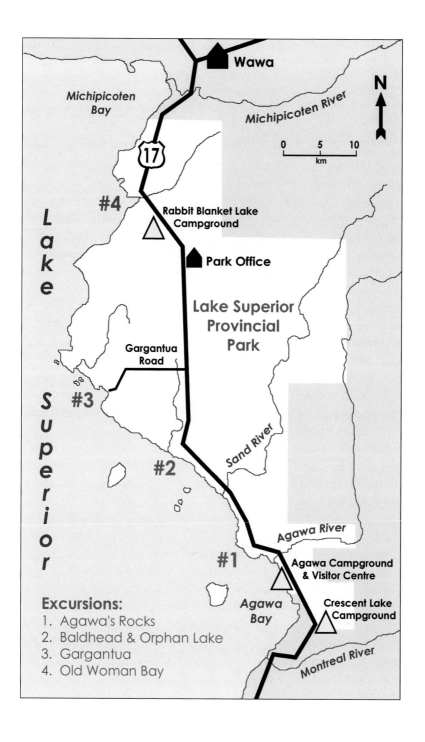

Wawa

Michipicoten
Bay

Michipicoten River

N

0   5   10
km

17

Lake

#4

Rabbit Blanket Lake
Campground

Park Office

Lake Superior
Provincial
Park

Gargantua
Road

Superior

#3

#2

Sand River

Agawa River

#1

Agawa Campground
& Visitor Centre

Agawa
Bay

Crescent Lake
Campground

Excursions:
1. Agawa's Rocks
2. Baldhead & Orphan Lake
3. Gargantua
4. Old Woman Bay

Montreal River

have produced an excellent topographic map of the park that is an essential companion on these excursions. It may be purchased at the park office, the Agawa Bay Visitor Centre, and many outdoor stores across the province.

Access
- Take Hwy 17 northwest 125 km from Sault Ste. Marie or south 10 km from Wawa.
- Purchase a permit from one of the following stations:
- Agawa Bay campground and Visitor Centre (8 km from the south end of the park, 73 km from the north end)
- Day-use registration box at the Agawa Pictographs (15 km from the south, 66 km from the north)
- Gargantua Road backcountry registration box (43 km from the south, 38 from the north)
- Park office at Red Rock Lake (59 km from the south, 22 km from the north)
- Rabbit Blanket Lake campground (63 km from the south, 18 km from the north)
- Day-use registration box at Old Woman Bay (70 km from the south, 11 km from the north)
- Proceed to the access point listed at the start of each excursion.

Agawa's Rocks

The highlights of this excursion are the celebrated Native pictographs at Agawa Rock, the extraordinary talus caves on the Agawa section of the Coastal Trail, and the views from the clifftop lookouts above Sinclair Cove and the Agawa Islands. The paddling portion of the excursion can be omitted if lake conditions are ominous, as the hiking portion can be done independently. If the lake is benign, however, the paddle may be prolonged, and the offshore islands and shoals explored more extensively.

- Main Route: 5.5 km hike, 3—10 paddle
- Alternative(s): 6.5 km hike

Access
- Exit Hwy 17 west onto the Sinclair Cove and Agawa Pictographs access road (15 km from the south end of the park, 66 km from the north end). Follow the road 500 m past the main Pictographs parking lot to the parking area at the bottom of the hill and launch the boat at the at Sinclair Cove beach.

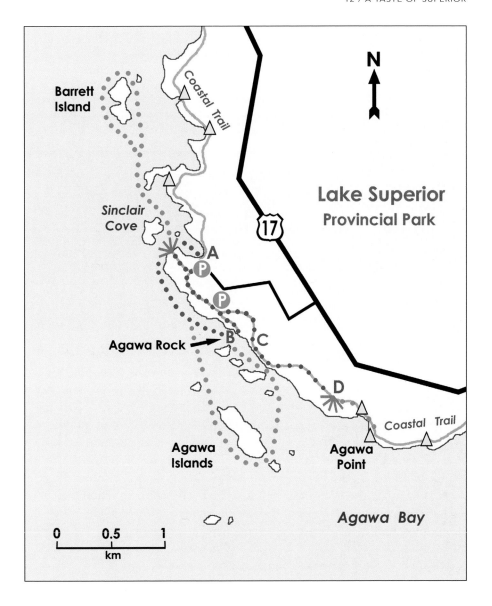

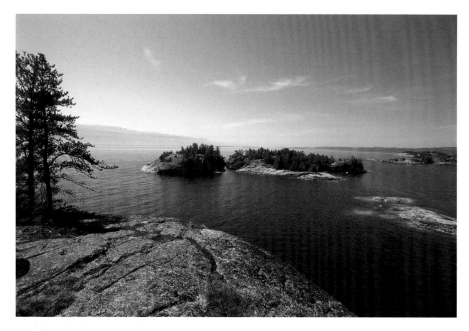

Lookout over Sinclair Cove

Route Description
1st Segment: Sinclair Cove, Agawa Rock and Offshore Islands (3–10 km paddle)

From the launch A paddle along the left-hand shoreline and follow it as it curves around the headland into the open lake. Sinclair Cove, like all the sheltered inlets along the north shore, was used by Native and early European travellers as a place to retreat from the fury of Lake Superior. During the nineteenth century the cove became a fishing station where catches were sorted and packed. Then, after the collapse of the fishery in the mid-twentieth century, it became a resting place again, this time for adventurers exploring the shoreline by canoe and kayak.

Continue south from the headland for 0.7 km, where Agawa Rock B will become obvious — a sheer slab of rock tilting slightly toward the lake, with a precarious ledge (and almost inevitably a group of tourists) at its base. This is the natural canvas for the Agawa Pictographs, a collection of red-ochre images painted by Native travellers to commemorate historical events and to honour their manitous. The park brochure, "Agawa Rock Pictographs," gives some historical background and discusses possible interpretations of the drawings. Many of the images have faded after centuries of erosion by water and ice, while others have disappeared altogether, erased by lichens or relinquished to the lake on chunks of fallen rock. Of the more than 100 images identified in the late 1800s by the site's first investigators, only about 35 are still visible today. Among them is a striking image of Mishepeshu and a canoe, believed to represent the historic four-day crossing of Lake Superior in the seventeenth century by chief Myeegun and his Ojibwe followers. Some images clearly depict creatures from the natural world, while others remain bewitchingly enigmatic.

From Agawa Rock return along the shoreline to the Sinclair Cove launch or, if time and lake conditions permit, paddle into the lake and explore the chain of offshore islands, beginning with the Agawa Islands just to the south of Agawa Rock and venturing as far as Barrett Island to the north.

2nd Segment: Coastal Trail from Sinclair Cove to the Agawa Islands Lookout (3 km hike)

At Sinclair Cove exchange your boat for a pair of hiking boots and pick up the Coastal Trail on the west side of the parking area. After about 25 m, a scenic side-trail exits to the right and scrambles steeply to the top of the rocky headland overlooking Sinclair Cove. Make your way back down the hill, turn right, and follow the Coastal Trail as it winds through the woods for 0.5 km to join the popular Agawa Rock Pictographs Trail. Turn right onto the Pictographs Trail and follow it a few metres to the next junction. From here it is possible to revisit the pictographs via the waterfront ledge. Otherwise, continue along the fork that cuts inland through a moss-lined passage (formed from an eroded dike of volcanic diabase rock) and loops back to the main parking lot. Shortly before the parking lot, the Coastal Trail departs to the right.

Note: Dogs are not permitted on the Agawa Rock Pictographs Trail, so anyone with a canine

Talus tunnels and caves on the Agawa Coastal Trail

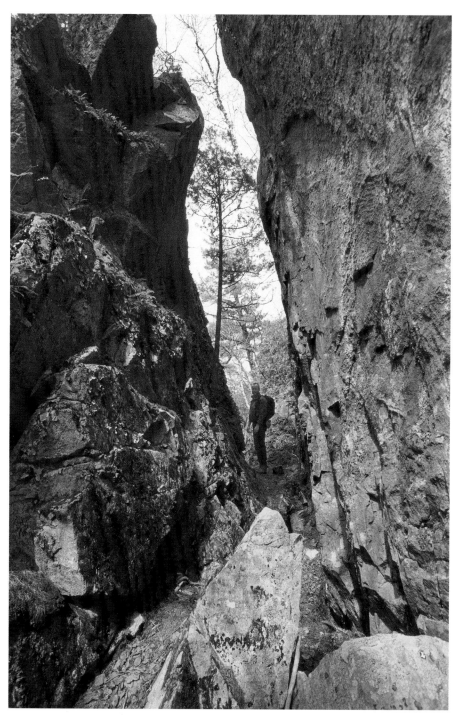

Above and right: Talus tunnels and caves on the Agawa Coastal Trail

companion should forgo this second look at the pictographs and make their way directly to the next leg of the hike.

From here the Agawa section of the Coastal Trail (a recent addition to the system opened in 2002) twists its way southward, passing behind Agawa Rock, then curving toward the water and following the shoreline toward the trail's southern terminus at Agawa Bay. There are many diversions along the way, both horizontal and vertical, making this section one of the most demanding in the Coastal Trail system. One diversion takes the trail through a massive field of talus C— enormous chunks of rock broken from ancient mountain cliffs and piled up at their base to form a jumble of caves and tunnels. The trail eventually climbs across an airy ridge to a height of land D overlooking the Agawa Islands, which makes an excellent place for a contemplative picnic lunch before you begin the homeward journey.

3rd Segment: Homeward (2.5 km hike)

Turn back from the lookout and follow the outward trail to the main Agawa Pictographs parking lot, then walk down the hill along the road for 500 m to your vehicle at Sinclair Cove.

Alternative: Omit the Paddle (6.5 km hike)

If wind and wave conditions make the exposed coastal paddle impossible, the main features of the excursion can be covered entirely by land via the Coastal Trail and its side-trails to the Sinclair Cove lookout and the Agawa Rock pictographs. If time permits an extended hike, continue 0.5 km south past the Agawa Islands lookout D and descend across a rocky beach to Agawa Point before turning back. Beyond Agawa Point the trail becomes less interesting as it turns away from the water and approaches the highway toward Agawa Bay.

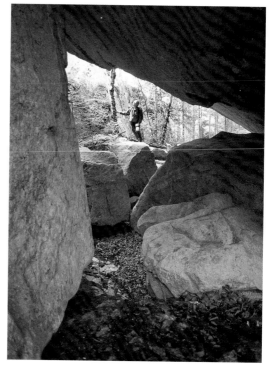

Baldhead and Orphan Lake

The Orphan Lake Trail is one of Lake Superior Provincial Park's most varied and challenging day-hiking trails. It visits a tranquil inland lake, a forest fire burnout area, a magnificent cobble beach, a tumbling river with several small waterfalls, and two splendid lookouts. The trail is usually approached from the parking lot beside Hwy 17, but this excursion approaches it from the water, exploring a 4 km section of coastline along the way.

- Main Route: 6 km hike, 8 km paddle
- Alternative(s): 8-14 km hike

Access

- Exit Hwy 17 at the Coldwater River (30 km from the south end of the park, 51 km from the north end) and park along the sandy track on the west side of the highway just north of the bridge. From here it is a short (100 m) portage to the beach to launch your canoe or kayak.

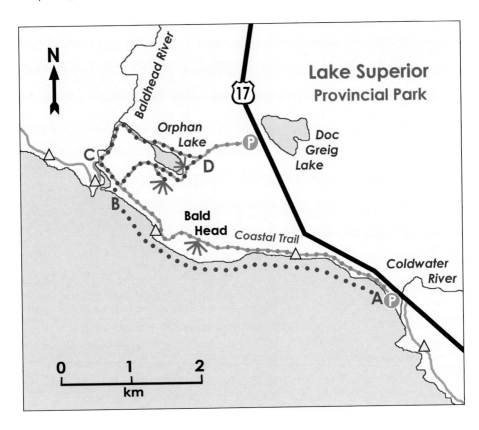

Twisted rock formations along the Baldhead coastline

Route Description
1st Segment: Coldwater River to Baldhead River (4 km paddle)

Paddle northwest from the launch A. The first 1.5 km of shoreline is gentle, but as it curves around the headland the contours become steeper, with cliffs and crevices plunging into the lake and Bald Head looming above them. Along the shore the rocks have been battered smooth by waves and ice. Running through the soft pinks and greys of the ancient granite are ribbons of black volcanic rock and brilliant patches of white quartz, all twisted into fascinating patterns. Around the headland lies the long crescent of Baldhead Beach B at the mouth of the Baldhead River. The "beach" consists entirely of variously sized cobbles; polished and rounded by centuries of tumbling, it resembles a basket of multicoloured eggs. Pull your boat ashore here (far up the beach out of reach of the surf!) and continue on foot.

2nd Segment: Orphan Lake Trail (6 km hike)

Pick up the hiking trail at the north end of Baldhead Beach and follow it as it winds upstream beside the Baldhead River. At the trail junction C the Coastal Trail crosses a bridge over the river and departs northward toward Beatty Cove. Take the right-hand, Orphan Lake Trail, and continue upstream (and breathlessly uphill!) past a series of pretty rapids and waterfalls to the western edge of Orphan Lake. Circling the lake, the trail climbs to another junction D. The left-hand fork leads to the parking lot on Hwy 17. Take the right-hand fork, which turns west to a clifftop lookout over Orphan Lake — a lovely place for a picnic lunch. The trail then descends

Baldhead coastline from the Orphan Lake side-trail lookout

to the lake, passing among the skeletons of trees charred in a forest fire started accidentally by visitors in 1998. In the open sunny soil, a tangle of new vegetation is flourishing, offering hope for the resiliency of nature in the face of human carelessness. A side-trail in the midst of the burnout climbs the hill to a lookout over the Bald Head coast — another splendid picnic spot. Once back on the main trail, it is only a short descent to your boat at Baldhead Beach B.

3rd Segment: Homeward (4 km paddle)
Return from Baldhead Beach south via the outward route along the shoreline to the launch at the mouth of the Coldwater River A.

Alternative 1: Omit the Paddle — Coastal Trail and Orphan Lake Trail (14 km hike)
The shoreline of this excursion is extremely exposed to prevailing westerly wind and waves, without offshore islands to offer shelter. If rough conditions prevent the coastal paddle, the excursion can be done entirely by land. From the parking area at the mouth of the Coldwater River follow the Coastal Trail north 4 km along the shoreline and over Bald Head to pick up the 2nd segment of the excursion at Baldhead Beach B. Return via the same route.

Alternative 2: Omit the Paddle — Orphan Lake Trail (8 km hike)

A pleasant day can also be spent hiking the Orphan Lake Trail, starting at the trailhead parking lot on the west side of Hwy 17 (32 km from the south end of the park, 49 km from the north end) and extending the hike either south from Baldhead Beach **B** for 1 km, climbing to lookouts on Bald Head, or north across the bridge over the Baldhead River **C**.

Gargantua's Bays, Capes and Islands

The Gargantua area pronounced "GAR-gan-twa" is rich in natural and human history. This excursion takes in some fine examples — the cliffs, beaches and rocky islands of its extraordinarily diverse landscape, and Devil's Chair and Devil's Warehouse Island, sites sacred to the peninsula's Native peoples.

Gargantua was shaped by the geological upheaval that accompanied the formation of the Midcontinental Rift about a billion years ago. Local faulting in the ancient bedrock created the cliffs and chasms found on Devil's Warehouse Island. The upwelling of volcanic material through the faults, and its subsequent erosion by water and ice, produced the labyrinth of crumpled rocks and craggy islands, including Devil's Chair, which are

177

Cobble beach at Gargantua Bay

found along the northwestern shoreline of Cape Gargantua. Erosion has also left behind several beaches — cobbled ones along Gargantua Bay, and sandy crescents at Gargantua Harbour and Warp Bay.

Gargantua likely acquired its name from the French voyageurs who paddled the Superior shore during the heyday of the fur trade. They called the peninsula "Gargantua" in hungry homage to King Gargantua, a fictitious monarch who was famous for hosting tremendous feasts. The names "Devil's Chair" and "Devil's Warehouse" were bestowed upon two of the peninsula's offshore islands by French missionaries in the eighteenth century. For Ojibwe travellers the islands were spiritual sites associated with their manitous, but the missionaries were bent on discrediting these manitous and winning Native people over to the Christian God. For the modern visitor, Gargantua's magnificent otherworldly atmosphere will almost certainly generate feelings of reverence — to which deity, perhaps, hardly matters!

• Main Route: 4—5 km hike, 12 km paddle
• Alternative(s): 0—18 km hike, 18+ km paddle

Access
- Exit Hwy 17 west onto the Gargantua Road (43 km from the south end of the park, 38 km from the north end). The 14 km road is very rough and twisty, so allow up to half an hour for the drive. Leave your vehicle in the parking area at Gargantua Bay and launch your boat from the cobble beach there.

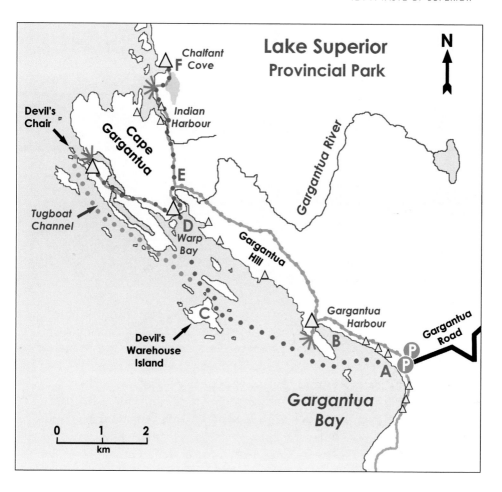

Route Description

1st Segment: Gargantua Bay to Warp Bay via Devil's Warehouse (6 km paddle)

Gargantua Bay, like many of the sheltered inlets along Superior's stormy northern shore, was a rest stop for Native and early European travellers. It became a commercial fishing station in the nineteenth and early twentieth centuries. A tiny community grew up around it, and the ruins of buildings from this era can still be seen in Gargantua Harbour B, the protected cove to the north of the launch site. In recent decades Gargantua Bay has become a mecca for tourists, with waterfront campsites housing weary paddlers overnight.

From the launch A paddle northwest between the mainland and Gargantua Island. The lighthouse on the island was manned by three generations of the Miron family from its establishment in 1889 until 1948 when it became automated. Past the lighthouse turn right and head toward

Approaching the cliffs of Devil's Warehouse Island

the cliffs of Devil's Warehouse Island **C**, which will be obvious among the scattered islands ahead. Devil's Warehouse was once a source of iron oxide mined to make the red-ochre pigment that Natives used for their rock art and body painting. The island's caves also housed a collection of birchbark scrolls that recorded events of historical and spiritual significance to Native peoples, before the scrolls vanished mysteriously in the 1970s. As you paddle along the base of the massive, lichen-encrusted rock face, it is not difficult to see why the site inspired such respect.

Leaving Devil's Warehouse Island, head north for 2 km past several small islands to the mainland at Warp Bay **D**, a sandy crescent at the mouth of the Gargantua River. Half a dozen backcountry campsites line the bay, and the shallow water is often sufficiently warm during the summer months to tempt you to a refreshing swim. Pull your kayak or canoe ashore on the beach and continue on foot.

A choice presents itself here between the two forks of the Coastal Trail. The eastern fork crosses over Cape Gargantua to Indian Harbour and Chalfant Cove. The western fork crosses the Cape to a headland overlooking Devil's Chair. Neither trail is overly long or rough, and both have splendid views, so the decision is not an easy one. More than one visit may be required!

180

2nd Segment, Western Option: Warp Bay to Devil's Chair (2 km hike)

Pick up the Coastal Trail at the bridge on the western side of the beach. It follows the cedar-lined shoreline of Pantagruel Bay (named after the legendary King Gargantua's drunkard son), then makes its way along a narrow headland, weaving between finger-like bays. Near the trail's northern terminus several side-trails lead to backcountry campsites, some tucked into crevices in the rock, others bordering a beach of black sand. These sites are worth visiting to admire the twisted rock formations and the views out over the lake. The main trail continues 100 m past the campsites and climbs to a lookout over Devil's Chair.

Devil's Chair, a spiky pyramid of volcanic rock, was a resting place for the beloved Ojibwe manitou Nanabosho. Natives traditionally left offerings of tobacco on the rock in the hope that Nanabosho would protect their journeys from the wrath of Lake Superior, a practice continued by voyageurs during the fur trade and even by adventurers plying the waters today. Devil's Chair is surrounded by Devil's Frying Pan, a ragged shelf of rock lying just below the water which can become a seething maelstrom of waves in rough weather.

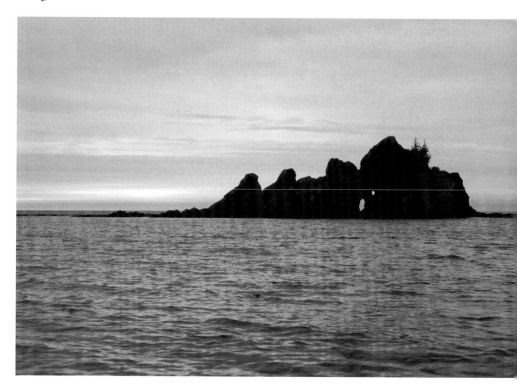

Storm approaching Devil's Chair

2nd Segment, Eastern Option: Warp Bay to Chalfant Cove (2.5 km hike)

Pick up the Coastal Trail on the eastern side of the beach and follow it upstream beside the Gargantua River for 0.7 km to a trail junction E. Turn left and continue northward as the trail winds across Cape Gargantua to Indian Harbour. It then follows the shoreline over several splendid rocky lookouts and an impressive marshland before emerging at its northern terminus on the beach at Chalfant Cove F.

3rd Segment: Homeward (2–2.5 km hike, 6 km paddle)

Return via the outward route along the Coastal Trail to Warp Bay D, then paddle back to the launch A at Gargantua Bay, either directly along the shoreline or, if time and conditions allow, further out into the lake to explore the string of shoals and islands offshore.

Alternative 1: Omit the Paddle (18 km hike)

In the event that wind and waves make the paddling portion of the excursion impossible, the excursion can be tackled as a full-day hike instead. Take the Coastal Trail north from the Gargantua Bay parking area. The trail follows the shoreline for 2.2 km to the beach at Gargantua Harbour B, where a short side-trail leads to a lookout at the top of the headland. From Gargantua Harbour the main trail cuts inland for 5 km on an old logging road, skirting the bulk of Gargantua Hill. The logging road is an easy but rather dull tramp through the woods, climbing behind the hill, then descending to the Gargantua River on the other side, where it again becomes more interesting as it approaches Warp Bay D. Pick up the 2nd segment of the excursion from Warp Bay, then return via the same route.

Alternative 2: Omit the Hike (18+ km paddle)

Gargantua's bays, capes and islands are perhaps most rewardingly experienced from the perspective of the water. So, if weather permits, the paddling portion of the excursion can be extended and the terrestrial portion restricted to just a few brief landings to stretch the legs. From Devil's Warehouse Island C continue paddling northwest for 4 km along Tugboat Channel to admire the shoreline's volcanic rocks and shoals, then curve around the top of the headland, where Devil's Chair will be immediately visible. After a close-up look at the Chair (where extreme caution must be exercised to avoid sizzling in the Devil's Frying Pan) it may be possible, depending on the lake conditions, to continue north around Cape Gargantua to explore Indian Harbour and Chalfant Cove. Otherwise, paddle back down Tugboat Channel and return to the launch A at Gargantua Bay, visiting Warp Bay D and Gargantua Harbour D along the way.

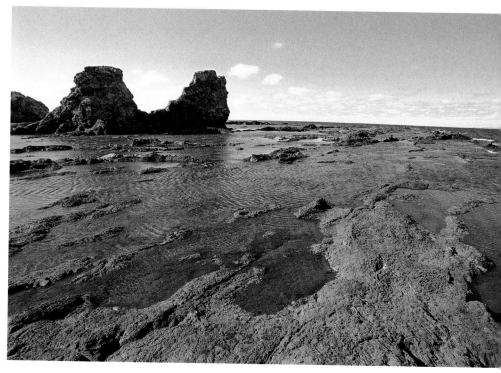

Devil's Frying Pan

Old Woman Bay and Brûlé Harbour

The natural features found along this route include the spectacular cliffs of Old Woman Bay, the placid inlets of Brûlé Harbour, and the cobble beaches scattered halfway up the surrounding hills. Interesting fragments of human history are woven into the natural landscape — Nokomis, the Ojibwe grandmother who gave Old Woman Bay her name; Étienne Brûlé, the maverick French explorer from which Brûlé Harbour gets its name; and the ancient Pukaskwa pits whose origin and purpose remain a mystery.

- Main Route: 5 km hike, 13–15 km paddle
- Alternative: 5 km hike

Access

- Exit on the west side of Hwy 17 into the Old Woman Bay parking lot (70 km from the south end of the park, 11 km from the north end), where there are toilet facilities, a picnic area and a day-use permit box.

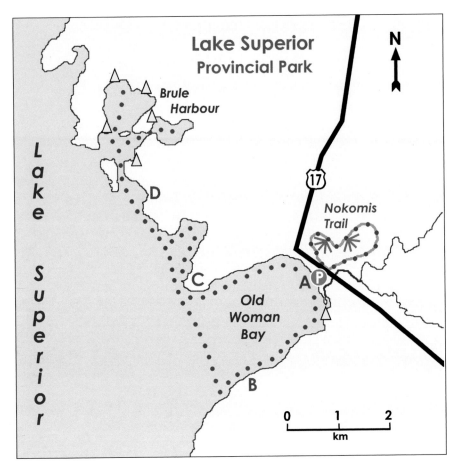

Route Description
1st Segment: Nokomis Trail (5 km hike)

From the parking area, cross Hwy 17 to the Nokomis Trailhead. The trail, a popular loop with several interpretive panels, heads inland from the highway along the Old Woman River valley for 0.7 km. Then, turning away from the valley, it climbs upward, gently at first then steeply to the top of a ridge.

During the climb the trail crosses outcroppings of smooth round rocks resembling those along the wave-battered shore of Lake Superior, but dry and encrusted with lichens. These are the "raised cobble beaches" commonly found on Superior's hillsides — the successive shorelines left behind as Lake Superior receded after the last period of glaciation ended some 10,000 years ago. Filled with glacial meltwater, the lake was at one time as much as 70 m higher than it is today, and the level of the land was lower, having been compressed by the weight of as much as 2 km of ice for tens of thousands of years. As the ice retreated north, the meltwater drained away and the land rebounded, gradually diminishing the volume of the lake to its present (though still impressive!) size.

Amid the ancient beaches can be found the curious formations known as Pukaskwa (pronounced "PUCK-a-saw") pits — circular depressions ringed by low walls of cobbles. The pits are thought to have been formed by Native people many centuries ago; estimates of their age range from several hundred to several thousand years. There is much speculation about the purpose of the pits. They may have been utilitarian structures like fireplaces, food caches or hunting blinds, or they may have been spiritual and ceremonial sites.

At the top of the ridge several rocky promontories offer splendid lookouts, the first toward the east down the Old Woman River valley and the others to the west over Old Woman Bay. The "old woman" is Nokomis, after whom the trail is named. She is Nanabosho's grandmother, the Ojibwe's nurturing female figure who represents fertility and growth. Her face is said to be visible in the shadows of the cliffs across the bay.

From the ridge the trail winds steeply down the hill and returns to the trailhead and the parking lot across the highway.

Nokomis Trail lookout over Old Woman Bay

2nd Segment: Old Woman Bay to Brûlé Harbour (8–10 km paddle)

Launch your canoe or kayak from the beach **A** into Old Woman Bay. Keeping the shore to your left, paddle along the edge of the cliff **B**. At close proximity, it towers dizzyingly above your boat. The cliff developed along a crack in the bedrock known as the Red River Fault. Shifts in the Earth's crust caused the rock on the west side of the fault to become displaced 7 km southward and down, into the lake, leaving a sheer slab of rock rising 150 m out of the water on the east side.

Where the cliff begins to subside, paddle across Old Woman Bay to the opposite side **C** and continue northward along the shoreline, where the contours are gentler and the rocky headlands are interspersed with cobble beaches. Many of these beaches stretch hundreds of metres back from the water (and hundreds of centuries back in time) and Pukaskwa pits are abundant among the cobbles. One particularly fine example, containing almost a dozen rings, may be found on the beach just beyond a large outcrop of reddish rock **D**.

Paddle through the channel to the right of Entrance Island into Brûlé Harbour, whose sheltered arms provide an hour's peaceful paddling and some lovely picnic sites.

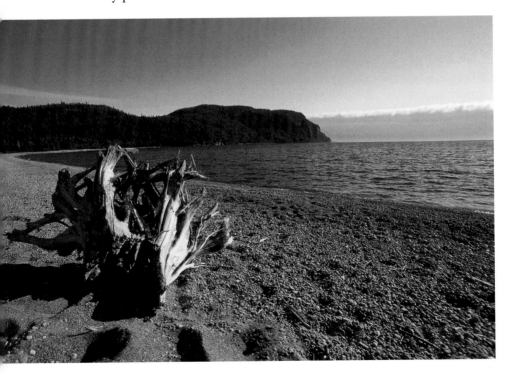

Beach at Old Woman Bay

Brûlé Harbour is named after Étienne Brûlé who was, perhaps, the first European to see Lake Superior. A protégé of famous seventeenth century explorer Samuel de Champlain, Brûlé was sent into the Ontario wilderness to scout travel routes and learn the language and customs of the Native people who lived there. From 1610 to 1621 (age 18–29) he travelled extensively — west along the Ottawa–Mattawa–French River route into Georgian Bay and onward as far as Lake Superior, and also south through lakes Ontario and Erie into the Susquehanna River and Chesapeake Bay. His association with the Native people became so intimate that he spent much of the 1620s living with Huron and Iroquois tribes, acting as interpreter and negotiator between the Natives and the French. Eventually his disenchantment with his French compatriots became so complete that he returned to Quebec to pilot the English fleet that captured Champlain's forces at Quebec City in 1629. He then retired to the wilderness and spent his remaining years among the Hurons — at whose hands, following a dispute, he met his death in 1632 at the age of 40.

3rd Segment: Homeward (5 km paddle)
From Brûlé Harbour return along the shoreline to Old Woman Bay and follow the northern shore of the bay back to the beach A.

Alternative: Omit the Paddle
If wind and waves prevent the exposed coastal paddle, the Nokomis Trail makes a leisurely morning's hike, leaving the afternoon free for one of several other options. The Michipicoten section of the Voyageur Trail provides some splendid hiking possibilities and, when Lake Superior is too rough, paddling may still be possible on one of the calmer inland lakes (see Other Paddling & Hiking Opportunities below). A few kilometres to the north of the park lie the towns of Michipicoten River and Wawa, where a gentle stroll may come as a pleasant change of pace after the rugged hiking of the Coastal Trail.

Other Hiking & Paddling Opportunities

Lake Superior Provincial Park, with 128 km of hiking trails, 150 km of maintained inland paddling routes and 120 km of Lake Superior coastline, boasts some of the finest hiking and paddling opportunities in the province. The excursions in this chapter visit several of the highlights, but many others are possible.

Hiking

- Peat Mountain Trail: an 11 km loop, accessed from the Rabbit Blanket Lake campground, which climbs 150 m to the summit of Peat Mountain and offers splendid views to the west over Foam Lake toward Lake Superior and east over the interior hills and valleys.
- South Old Woman Trail: a 2.5 km cedar-lined loop following the tumbling course of the South Old Woman River.
- Trapper's Trail: a 1.5 km loop along the shore of Rustle Lake which follows a trail that was formerly a trapline (from the 1930s to 1970s) and now treats the hiker to a floating boardwalk across a marshland.
- Pinguisibi Trail: a 6 km (return) linear trail that follows the Sand River upstream past a series of waterfalls and rapids.
- Awausee Trail: a 10 km loop that climbs from the Agawa River to the ridge 200 metres above, where there are impressive vistas eastward down the Agawa River Valley and westward over Agawa Bay.
- Towab Trail: a linear trail that descends through a deciduous woodland to Burnt Rock Pool (6 km return, an easy day-hike), and then follows the Agawa River eastward to Agawa Falls, which cascades 25 metres over a rocky ledge (24 km return, intended as a backpacking hike).
- Crescent Lake Trail: a 2 km loop, starting at the Crescent Lake campground, which winds through a mature birch and pine forest and along the shores of several small lakes.
- Coastal Trail: a magnificent and challenging linear trail that follows the Lake Superior shoreline for 63 km from Agawa Bay in the south to Chalfant Cove and Devil's Chair in the north. The route takes 5–7 days (one-way) as a backpacking trip, but many of the trail's sections (several of which are covered in this chapter) can be done as day-hikes from access points along Hwy 17.
- The Michipicoten Section of the Voyageur Trail (a magnificent long-distance hiking trail that, when finished, will run 1100 km along the northern shores of lakes Huron and Superior from Manitoulin Island to Thunder Bay): this section of the Voyageur Trail begins at the northern boundary of the park, continues north along the coast to the Michipicoten River and then turns inland to follow the Magpie River Valley past Magpie Falls to the town of Wawa. For more information contact the Voyageur Trail Association at 1-877-393-4003, www3.sympatico.ca/voyageur.trail.

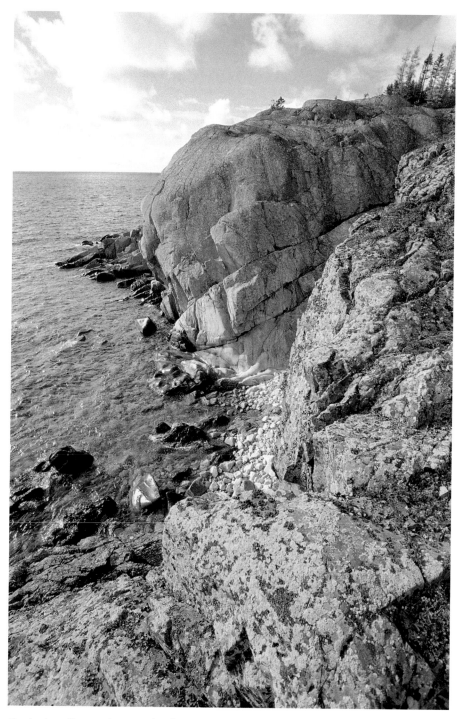

Rocky headline at the mouth of Old Woman Bay

Raised cobble beach near Brûlé Harbour

Paddling

Paddling possibilities in Lake Superior Provincial Park are plentiful, but most require solid paddling skills to safely handle the demanding conditions.

The Lake Superior shoreline, 120 km of which runs through the park, is notorious for its wind, waves, cold and fog, and paddlers can expect to be shore-bound for one out of every three or four days. However, when the lake is feeling cooperative, a coastal paddle is a wonderful experience for the seasoned paddler. Access points include Old Woman Bay in the north, and Agawa Bay, Katherine Cove or Sinclair Cove in the south.

Inland, there are many lakes and rivers to explore, ranging from short day-trips to multi-day excursions. However, the rugged terrain and steep topography produce some wild whitewater and necessitate frequent portaging along many of the routes. The 56 km Sand River, for instance, has 29 portages (1 portage every 2 km, ranging from a few metres to 1100 m) and many Class I and II rapids to run, as it plummets from the interior highlands to the Superior shore.

Practical Information

Lake Superior Provincial Park

- Park Season: open from early May to late October.
- Park Permit: required for all Lake Superior Provincial Park users. Day-use and backcountry permits are available from many locations in the park during the summer season (see Access section at the beginning of this chapter), and at the park office during the off-season.
- Camping: a total of 235 drive-in campsites with comfort stations,

telephones and trailer facilities are available at the Agawa Bay campground near the south end of the park, and at the Rabbit Blanket Lake campground toward the north end of the park. The Crescent Lake campground at the park's southern border has 39 drive-in sites and more primitive facilities. Although availability is not usually such a problem as it is in provincial parks further south, in the summer months it is advisable to book campsites in advance. Lake Superior Park also has 275 interior campsites scattered on the shorelines of the park's interior waterways and along the Lake Superior coast.

- Cans and bottles are banned in the Lake Superior Provincial Park interior. This ban includes all lakes and day-use trails as well as interior campsites, but does not include the park campgrounds or day-use areas along Hwy 17.
- Information: park office (705) 856-2284, Ontario Parks Reservation Service 1-888-668-7275, www.ontarioparks.com.
- The Niijkiwenhwag (Friends of Lake Superior Provincial Park) is a non-profit association established in 1993 to assist park staff in providing educational programs and publications that promote public appreciation of the park's natural environment; contact the Friends at (705) 856-2284.

Cliffs of Old Woman Bay

Maps & Publications

- The Friends of Lake Superior Provincial Park have published an excellent topographic map, showing the park's hiking trails, paddling routes, portages and interior campsites, with elevations and points of interest indicated along the way. This map is essential for travelling in the park, and can be purchased at the park office or Agawa Bay Visitor Centre and at many outdoor stores across the province.
- A "Hiking Trails" pamphlet and a "Paddling Routes" brochure are available from the park office and Agawa Bay Visitor Centre. The park also publishes an annual Visitor Information Guide, available by mail or in person at many locations in the park.

Supplies, Accommodations & Attractions Outside the Park

- Basic supplies are available in the community of Montreal River Harbour, 12 km to the south of the park boundary. More extensive supplies and accommodations are available in Wawa, 10 km to the north of the park, and at locations along Hwy 17 toward Sault Ste. Marie in the south.
- Boat rentals and outfitting services: Canoes are available for rent during the summer season from the Agawa Bay and Rabbit Blanket Lake campgrounds. Naturally Superior Adventures in Michipicoten River just to the north of the park provides canoe and kayak rentals, outfitting services, accommodations and guided tours. For information contact (705) 856-2939 or 1-800-203-9092, www.naturallysuperior.com.
- Wawa Tourist Information Centre: (705) 856-2244 or 1-800-367-9292, www.wawa.ca.

Appendix I: Gear for Paddling & Hiking Excursions

An excursion that combines paddling and hiking requires a special collection of equipment to make the time in the boat and on the trail both safe and comfortable. Some items are stipulated by law. Others are dictated by common sense. And others are relative luxuries that can be brought along or left behind at the discretion of the individual excursion-goer.

Gear Required by Law

Canadian Coast Guard regulations governing small pleasure craft require canoes, kayaks and rowboats up to 6 metres in length to carry the following equipment:

An approved, correctly sized lifejacket or personal flotation device (PFD) for each person aboard.

Lifejackets and PFDs are intended to keep a person afloat in case of capsize. A lifejacket is designed to float an unconscious person into a face-up position in a variety of water conditions, whereas a PFD is designed to float a conscious person, keeping the head above water in relatively calm conditions. It will be obvious from these definitions that lifejackets provide greater buoyancy than PFDs and the greatest possible safety. They are mandatory on commercial vessels. For recreational paddlers, however, a PFD gives adequate protection in most circumstances, and has the advantage of being considerably less bulky. An "approved" PFD is one that meets the Canadian Coast Guard standards for method of construction and passes tests for flotation and durability. Not all PFDs sold in Canada are approved, so check the label before buying one.

Most PFDs have a vest-like design and are constructed from closed-cell foam encased in water-resistant fabric. Correctly sized, this construction provides the fit and buoyancy required by the boating regulations. Closed-cell foam comes in several grades, the higher grades being softer and less rigid than the lower grades. PFDs are typically designed with articulated panels, a zipper closure at the front or side reinforced by a buckle closure at the waist, and adjustable straps at the sides and shoulders. These features enable the wearer to cinch the PFD snugly around the upper body, ensuring the correct fit. When trying on a PFD, secure all the fastenings without over-tightening them. There should still be room to tighten or loosen the fastenings to accommodate the layers of clothing needed in different seasons. Have somebody pull upward on the shoulder straps. The PFD should stay close to the body and not "ride up" toward the face; this will enable the PFD to hold your mouth above water in case of emergency.

The most visible and therefore the safest PFDs are yellow, orange or red. Until recently these bright colours were the only ones approved by the Canadian Coast Guard. The regulations have been relaxed, however, and now allow more subdued shades of blue, green and grey.

In the final analysis the only PFD worth buying is the one that you will actually wear. The lightweight stylish vest on your body is infinitely better than the super-buoyant bulky jacket stuffed beneath your canoe seat; the dark blue PFD you aren't embarrassed to be seen in is preferable to the brilliant orange one tucked under the shock-cording of your kayak deck. In choosing a PFD, consider safety first, but select the one that is most comfortable and has the nifty extra features and the colour that appeals to you. When trying on a PFD, sit in the paddling position and mimic the movement of paddling. Be sure that nothing chafes or pinches. Check that the armholes are large enough to allow full and free range of motion. Ensure that the length of the PFD is appropriate (short-waisted PFDs can be used in either kayaks or canoes, but longer PFDs are generally only suitable for a canoe). Women, especially generously endowed ones, may appreciate a PFD specifically designed to fit a woman's figure. Gadget and snack-food junkies will welcome the pockets and clips that are commonly incorporated into the design of PFDs. Reflective tape will appeal to the night owl. As in most of life's important purchases, you generally get what you pay for in a PFD, so buy the best quality you can afford. And then wear it — every time, all the time, until it becomes as second nature as fastening your seatbelt when you get into the car.

In addition to the vest-style PFD, Coast Guard regulations allow inflatable PFDs (which lie smoothly against the body until needed, and are then inflated with compressed carbon dioxide) and closed-cell foam jackets (which look like ordinary jackets and provide water-repellency and warmth in cooler weather, but incorporate floatation panels into the design).

PFDs should be allowed to dry thoroughly after use, and should be stored in a well-ventilated place away from direct sunlight and heat. They should not be used to kneel on or be subjected to any other sort of compression. Check your PFD regularly for tears, punctures and mildew, and test the buoyancy of the PFD annually by wearing it in the water. Even well-cared-for PFDs will have to be replaced eventually — every 5–10 years, depending on how much they are used. Finally, never alter the PFD in any way by removing or adding features, as any alteration automatically voids the Coast Guard approval.

For more information about PFDs, contact the Canadian Coast Guard Office of Boating Safety at 1-800-267-6687, www.ccg-gcc.gc.ca/obs-bsn/sbg-gsn/main_e.htm.

Manual propelling device (i.e., paddle, set of oars)

This seems a ridiculously obvious requirement for a canoe, kayak or rowboat, but keep in mind that the regulations also apply to other small vessels like sailboats and motorboats, whose operators might not otherwise think to equip their boat with a paddle. Surprisingly, the boating regulations do not require a spare paddle. Even if not legally required, a spare should be part of your equipment list in case your main paddle becomes lost or broken. The spare should be easily accessible in an emergency, so do not lash it to the canoe thwarts or stow it in the kayak bulkhead.

Buoyant heaving line at least 15 metres long

This requirement is simply a length of floating rope that may be used to tow a boat or haul in a swimmer who has fallen overboard. For maximum throw, it is useful to have a weighted (but buoyant!) object attached to one end of the rope. The basic version of the heaving line is the type of yellow nylon rope that is readily and inexpensively available from any hardware store. More sophisticated versions that include a throwing bag are available at outdoor stores.

Bailer or manual water pump

Rough conditions or damage to your boat may result in water getting aboard, so a reliable means of getting rid of that water is essential. According to the regulations a bailer must be made of metal or plastic and have a volume of at least 750 ml with a minimum opening of 65 cm^2. A suitable container may be purchased from any hardware or household supplies store (consider using, for instance, a plastic jug designed to hold milk-bags).

Alternatively, you could fashion a bailer from a bleach bottle by screwing the cap on tightly and cutting out the bottom. If a pump is used instead of a bailer it must be able to reach over the edge of the boat to discharge the water. Foot-operated and hand-operated pumps are available, the latter being the more common. The pump or bailer should be easily accessible in the boat — clipped to a thwart in the canoe or tucked under the shock-cording on the kayak deck. A useful supplementary item for clearing out the last drops of water (and also sand and dirt) is a large sponge, which can be stored inside the bailer until needed.

Sound-signalling device (i.e., whistle or horn)

The whistle required by the boating regulations should be part of the standard equipment to be carried both on the water and on land. It can be clipped to the PFD, backpack or item of clothing where it is easily accessible. Whistles are widely available at outdoor and hardware stores. Most are made of plastic and are not expensive. You should buy the loudest possible whistle so that its sound will carry furthest in an emergency. For signalling purposes the generally accepted code is:

- THREE short, sharp whistle blasts, repeated frequently, signal an emergency.
- TWO whistle blasts alert travel companions without alarming them, and can also be a request for them to come to you.
- ONE whistle blast is the typical reply to a TWO- or THREE-blast signal, to acknowledge that the signal has been heard. A single blast can also be used to mean "Stop!" or can just be a means of communicating the whereabouts of various members of a group. In order to avoid confusion when travelling with a group, be sure to discuss and agree upon the whistle code before setting out.

Navigation light if the boat is operated after sunset or before sunrise

A waterproof flashlight fulfills this requirement. It can be used for illumination both in the boat and on shore, and also for signalling in case of emergencies (3 short flashes, like 3 whistle blasts, indicate an SOS). Another alternative for emergency signalling is a flare, which is more highly visible to potential rescuers than a flashlight beam. Available from most outdoor stores, flares range in sophistication according to their brightness, altitude and burn time. Some are simple hand-held devices; others are fired from pistols.

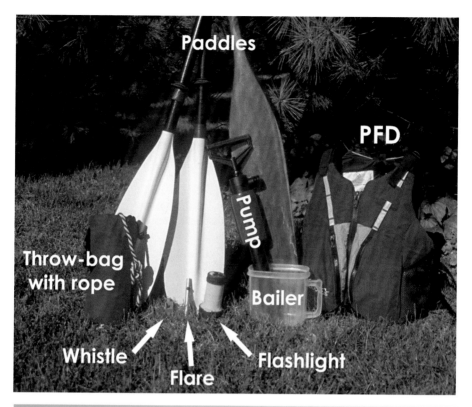

Paddles

PFD

Pump

Throw-bag with rope

Bailer

Whistle

Flare

Flashlight

Other Necessary Gear

While not required by law, common sense suggests that the following items be included among the equipment for any hiking and paddling excursion:

Hiking Boots & Boating Shoes

A good hiking boot on the trail is akin to a PFD in the boat — it protects the wearer against injury and keeps the feet comfortable and the ankles supported over rough terrain. Fit is absolutely critical in selecting a pair of boots. Pay absolutely no attention to the appearance of the boots or their price until the fit is perfect. Only then, if you are fortunate enough to find more than one comfortable pair, should you consider style or cost. Be prepared to pay at least $200 for good-quality boots; the investment will be handsomely repaid in the many hours of trouble-free hiking that you will enjoy. Shop at a reputable outdoor store that will have the best selection and most knowledgeable salespeople. Take along the types of socks you typically wear when hiking (i.e., a thin liner and a heavier outer sock), and if you normally need orthotic inserts or arch supports, bring them to check their fit inside the boot. Try on as many pairs as possible and spend a few minutes walking in each of them. Most outdoor stores will have an incline ramp and mock outdoor surfaces to test the boots under a variety of "natural" conditions. Be sure that the heels do not rub and the toes do not press against the boot when you walk up and down hills. The traditional full-grain leather boot is still among the most durable and supportive on the market, though it often feels stiff when new. Boots constructed from modern synthetic materials can be lightweight, waterproof and immediately comfortable, but they are sometimes less durable and more difficult to maintain.

No matter which type of boots you select, be sure to allow adequate time for breaking them in. Wear new boots around the house for brief periods to start, then around the block to walk the dog or down the street to do the shopping, and then for a few gentle hikes before undertaking a really serious excursion over rugged terrain. Pay attention to the manufacturer's care instructions with respect to cleaning, protecting and waterproofing the boots so that they will stand up to long-term use.

In order to minimize gear it may be tempting to take hiking boots as your only footwear on a hiking and paddling excursion. This temptation should be resisted! Hiking boots quickly become uncomfortable in a canoe, and in a kayak are virtually impossible. Bare feet in the boat may be acceptable in warmer weather, but your feet should be protected during launches and landings. A slip-on shoe, waterproof sandal or neoprene bootie will give the comfort, flexibility and protection you will need for the boating segment of the excursion, and may be packed away with the PFD and left in your boat during the hiking segment.

Backpack & Drybag

A backpack is essential during the hiking portion of an excursion to carry the supplies that may be needed on the trail. Packs vary in volume from small day-packs to mid-sized "weekend" packs to enormous "expedition" packs. Always carry a pack that is slightly larger than you think you will need, so that it will comfortably accommodate the day's food and water, emergency supplies and optional gear without stressing the seams or interfering with the zippers, and without having to be completely unpacked for you to get something at the bottom. Unless your needs are extremely modest, the standard day-pack (25–35 litre) is probably too small, and in any case the hip-belt that accompanies most day-packs is inadequate. A mid-volume (35–50 litre) pack is usually better suited to the needs of a day-long excursion.

Fit and comfort are critical in selecting the appropriate pack. A tall design correctly sized for the length of the back keeps the pack's weight well balanced and snug against the body, making it more comfortable than a boxy-shaped pack that tends to hang from the shoulders. The pack should have a wide, padded hip-belt to transfer most of its weight away from the vulnerable spine and shoulders onto the sturdier hips. It should have adjustable straps on the shoulders and sides so that it can be cinched close to the body. Good-quality packs are typically constructed from durable fabrics like Cordura®, packcloth or ripstop nylon, reinforced in high-stress areas and fitted with reliable zippers, buckles and drawstrings. As with all important purchases, a quality name-brand pack purchased from a reputable outdoor store will be worth the additional cost, ensuring years of comfortable, trouble-free use.

For the paddling portion of the excursion a drybag is a useful addition to the day's equipment. Made from polyvinyl chloride (PVC) or urethane-coated fabric, drybags are top-loading sacks that seal with a roll-down closure system to keep their contents dry. Many come equipped with a carrying strap or a shoulder harness resembling that of a backpack to make portaging more comfortable. Select a size that will hold all the gear not carried in the hiking backpack, including the PFDs, the boat's emergency supplies and boating footwear. A 40–60 litre capacity will be adequate for a modest load, but bags up to 125 litres are available for larger loads and can even accommodate the backpack in addition to the boating gear for a single load over a portage. The drybag can be tucked under the overturned canoe or into the kayak bulkhead for storage during the hiking portion of your excursion.

Maps & Navigation Tools

The maps included in this book are illustrative only, intended to give a rough overview of each excursion route. For accurate navigation, maps containing detailed topographic information about route locations are available commercially, and should be purchased and consulted along the way. The most durable maps are printed on tyvek, an expensive but tough waterproof material that will stand up to repeated use in rough conditions. The smooth texture of tyvek makes it difficult to write on. Standard paper maps are less expensive but also considerably less durable, tending to fade and to tear easily along fold-lines, especially if they become damp. Paper maps can be treated with waterproofing compounds to extend their life or, for the technologically adept, it is possible to scan relevant sections of paper maps, then print and laminate them for protection.

A simple compass—and the knowledge to use it correctly—is all that is required to translate the map's two-dimensional features onto the three-dimensional landscape, and vice versa. The compass should have high-quality components that enable the magnetic needle to pivot smoothly and reliably to the correct orientation. It should also have a 360° bezel and a transparent baseplate with navigational markings to align the compass properly with the map. Additional features are available in more sophisticated and expensive models, but are not always necessary.

A GPS can assist with navigation and can also provide hours of entertainment along the way, but it should never be used as the sole navigation tool to the exclusion of a map and compass.

Books about basic navigation are widely available, and courses — ranging from casual half-day seminars to intensive weekend training sessions — are offered by many community colleges and outdoor education centres.

Food & Water

The exertions of a day-long hiking and paddling trips demand an adequate supply of food and fluid to maintain needed levels of energy and hydration.

A hearty picnic lunch and several snacks will supply the necessary food energy. The ingredients should be rich in carbohydrates — things like granola bars, crackers, cookies, breads and fruits — which break down into the essential sugars that provide the calories to sustain hiking and paddling activities. The menu should also include some protein and fat — cheese, peanut butter, hard-boiled eggs, meat — which break down more slowly and provide slow-release calories for sustained physical activity. Trail mixes of GORP (Good Old Raisins and Peanuts) or more exotic blends including dried fruit, nuts, seeds and grains deliver combinations of carbohydrates, proteins and fats that make wonderfully easy and tasty snacks.

Water is the most obvious means of replenishing the body's fluid supply. During normal activity the body loses about one to three litres of fluid a day through perspiration and respiration. Strenuous exercise, especially in hot weather, can increase fluid loss to as much as three litres of fluid per hour. If the body loses water at a rate faster than it is able to absorb water from drinking, dehydration may result. Symptoms include thirst, fatigue, loss of coordination, lightheadedness, irritability and confusion. In extreme cases the cardiovascular system becomes impaired and loss of consciousness may result. By the time the hiker feels thirsty, mild dehydration has already set in, and it is then difficult to drink enough fluid to replenish the body's supply. It is important, therefore, to begin drinking before becoming thirsty. In fact, a wise practice is to drink at least half a litre of water before beginning a hike and continue sipping at the rate of about one litre per hour. The most convenient way of doing this is to carry a hydration bladder in the backpack with a hose that clips to the shoulder strap and a bite valve that releases water whenever a sip is taken. The alternative is to carry bottled water in a belt pack or in your hand. Do not leave it in your backpack, as you will be disinclined to stop and remove the pack to take a drink as often as you should. Although paddling is not generally as fluid-depleting as hiking, fluid loss is exacerbated by exposure to wind, sun and light reflected off the water, so frequent drinking is still recommended.

Loss of fluid through perspiration is accompanied by loss of electrolytes (salts), which should also be replenished during strenuous exercise. A salty snack will accomplish this, or a sports drink that contains added sodium to help restore the balance. Fruit juice, either concentrated or diluted in water, provides a welcome energy boost from the fruit sugars it contains. It is best to avoid caffeinated drinks, soft drinks and alcohol, as the body's processing of these drinks actually depletes rather than augments fluid levels. In chilly weather when perspiration is minimal, however, a thermos of tea or coffee can be very comforting.

Emergency Supplies
- Extra carbohydrate-rich food and a sweet drink (juicebox or package of flavoured drink crystals) for an energy boost.
- Extra clothing for warmth and rain protection: spare socks, fleece sweater, waterproof/windproof shell.
- Whistle and flashlight for emergency signalling (see "Required Gear").
- Matches (in a watertight container) for starting a fire.
- Space-blanket: made from lightweight plastic-metal fabric that helps retain heat and prevent hypothermia.
- First aid kit: pre-packaged kits are available from outdoor stores, or the ingredients can be purchased separately from a pharmacy and assembled in a small waterproof container. The kit should include an assortment of bandaging materials (several sizes of bandaids, a sterile gauze roll or squares, adhesive tape), disinfectant (antiseptic towelettes, alcohol pads, iodine wipes, hydrogen peroxide), antibiotic ointment, analgesic medication (ASA, acetaminophen or ibuprofen, better known by their respective brand names Aspirin, Tylenol and Advil), scissors, a sharp blade and tweezers (these tools are usually included in a good-quality pocket knife), and a basic first aid manual.
- Paddle-float: for kayakers, this additional safety item provides a buoyant outrigger to steady the boat during self-rescue in the event of capsize. Paddle-floats are available in inflatable format (fold away easily when not in use but take time to inflate and are susceptible to puncture) or closed-cell foam (instantly ready but take up space when not in use).

- Personal identification and a list of emergency contact names and telephone numbers, sealed in some sort of watertight sleeve.

Essential Odds & Ends

Depending on the time of year and the weather conditions of the day, the following items should be considered essential protective gear:

- Sunglasses: to protect the eyes against strain, glare from reflected light and damage from ultraviolet light, wear high-quality sunglasses with glass or polycarbonate lenses and polarizing filters.
- Glasses: anyone dependent on corrective eyewear should carry a spare pair.
- Sunscreen: to protect the skin against the harmful effects of ultraviolet light (sunburn, skin aging, skin cancer and immune system suppression), use a generous amount of sunscreen with a sun protection factor (SPF) of at least 15.
- Lip balm: apply to protect lips against drying and damage from sun and wind.
- Bug spray or lotion: the most effective insect repellents contain DEET as the active ingredient. Because it is a toxic chemical, the maximum concentration of DEET currently permitted is 30%, which gives up to six hours of protection. Environmentally friendly citronella sprays are safer but not generally as effective and must be applied more frequently.
- Prescription drugs according to medical condition: puffers for asthma, anti-inflammatories for arthritis, antihistamines for insect-bite allergies, epinephrine for bee-sting allergies, insulin and sugar for diabetics. Be sure that other members of the excursion are aware of any potential medical problems and what to do if treatment is required.
- Hat to protect against sun, rain, cold or snow. Choose one with a chin strap to prevent loss in wind.

Optional Gear

The list of "optional" gear is virtually limitless, contingent upon the interests and perceived needs of the individual excursion-goer. Some people prefer to travel light and are prepared to endure the relative privations of a spartan load; they carry only the essential gear listed in the previous sections. Other people are gear gluttons, willing to carry as much equipment as they can cram into their boats and hoist into their backpacks. There is no right or wrong to the gear question, provided the benefits and drawbacks of light and heavy loads are considered in advance and the consequences borne with good humour. Among the optional gear might be included the following:

- Reading materials: hiking and paddling guidebooks for the excursion area, nature field-guides (birds, wildflowers, trees, rocks and minerals, etc.).
- Photography equipment: camera, lenses, filters, tripod, spare batteries and film, all sealed in protective waterproof containers.
- Trekking pole to transfer some of your weight to your arms and ease stress on knees during descents (look for a pole with an anti-shock spring in the tip and a comfortable hand-grip).
- Inflatable pad to provide a soft, dry seat for rest stops.
- Folding pocketknife or multi-tool with an appropriate collection of attachments (knives, scissors, files, tweezers, toothpick, screwdrivers, bottle opener).
- Duct-tape — remarkably useful for all sorts of on-the-spot repairs.
- Tissues, toilet paper or paper towels (the latter being the most absorbent and durable but perhaps less comfortable for tender bits of anatomy), handiwipes.
- Notebook and pen or pencil.
- Binoculars.
- Cell phone or satellite phone.

Anyone undertaking paddling and hiking excursions on a regular basis will find it useful to prepare a permanent checklist of equipment. This can be done by hand and photocopied for each excursion, or — more conveniently — by computer, so that it can be stored, edited and printed as needed.

Appendix II: Excursions with Your Dog

There is no better companion on the hiking trail or in a boat than a faithful dog, and for the dog there is no happier way to spend a day than following a beloved human through the wilderness. It is a perfect partnership. It is not, however, the normal canine routine. So, to ensure that the excursion is a successful one, a few practical matters should be considered when hiking and paddling with your dog.

In the Boat
- Paddling with a dog is only possible if the dog is sufficiently well trained and accustomed to the boat that he will settle down and keep still, even in rough conditions or with enticements beckoning him overboard. The key is practice, preferably from an early age, beginning with brief paddles on placid lakes and graduating to extended periods in less predictable water.

Skye kayaking in Silent Lake (photo by Patrick Brobeck)

- Always take the dog for a walk before paddling to give him some exercise and a chance to relieve himself. Take breaks on land occasionally during the day so that he will not feel uncomfortably confined in the boat.
- The dog should be positioned in a central location. In a canoe this typically means on the floor ahead of the stern paddler. This keeps the dog's weight in an appropriate position. It also enables the paddler to watch the dog's movements and compensate for any shift in weight, and to restrain the dog should that become necessary. In a kayak, positioning is more problematic. Some people put their dog between their legs in the cockpit, but unless the cockpit is very spacious this arrangement quickly leads to cramped legs and a restless dog. Other people put the dog in a hatch, usually to the rear of the cockpit. As it is impossible to see or control the dog in this position, this arrangement is only possible with an extremely well-behaved dog. It also leaves the hatch open to the elements, exposing the boat to potential danger in rough water. Kayaking with a dog, therefore, is something most people choose to avoid.
- Warmth can be a consideration when paddling in cooler weather, as the dog is not generating heat from exercise while he is lying in a boat. He may require a jacket or light fleece blanket, and he should have something to lie on, both for warmth and for cushioning. A blanket, towel or mat may be used, although these tend to become saturated and consequently useless. A better (though considerably more expensive!) alternative is an inflatable Therm-a-Rest, as it can be easily dried and rolled out of the way when not in use. It should be encased in a lightweight covering to protect it from damage and dirt.

On the Trail

- Hiking requires the same general level of fitness for a dog as it does for his owner. A couch-potato will suffer from stresses and strains after an unaccustomed long hike, so maintain a sensible routine of regular exercise year-round in preparation.
- Provincial and national parks require that a dog be kept on a leash not exceeding 2 metres. The law is designed to protect wildlife from roving dogs and other hikers from disturbance, and also to keep the dog safe from accident and injury. Some parks, especially busy ones in southern Ontario, are strict about enforcement, conducting routine patrols along their trails, while others, especially in more remote areas in the north, are more forgiving of well-behaved off-leash dogs.
- When hiking with a dog on the leash, avoid the extendable style, which can easily become tangled in the undergrowth. Opt instead for a 2-metre nylon or soft leather leash. A haltie is an excellent device to prevent an excited dog from pulling on the leash, although it is best to get the dog accustomed to it at home before setting out on a wilderness excursion.

Energy Requirements

- Consider that the dog's normal routine is to sleep for much of the day, with a couple of short walks under relatively controlled conditions. On a wilderness hiking trail, especially off the leash, the dog may lose more than half his normal sleeping time and expend more than twice his normal energy, so appropriate adjustments should be made to his diet. An active dog hiking for the day will require as much as 50% more food, which should be given at frequent intervals. So along with your picnic, pack a small plastic bag of kibble ("lunch" will soon become one of the dog's favourite words!) and several extra biscuits for snacks along the trail.
- To avoid fatigue on extended trips, try to alternate hiking days and paddling days, beginning with a hiking day to allow the dog to burn off steam. The schedule of hiking and paddling should be adjusted on subsequent days to keep a balance of exercise and rest suited to the dog's temperament and physical capabilities.

Safety Considerations

- Safety regulations in a boat require its human occupants to have a PFD. Lifejackets for dogs are also available from many outdoor stores. Be sure the fit is appropriate and that the dog is accustomed to wearing it so he is comfortable and properly protected in the boat.
- The dog's vaccinations should be kept up to date for protection against preventable diseases while travelling. In addition to the standard canine

vaccine including rabies, consider adding vaccines against lyme disease (a bacterial disease carried by ticks) and leptospirosis (a bacterial disease transmitted in infected urine) if visiting high-risk areas.

- A day on a rough hiking trail can result in cuts, abrasions, soft-tissue bruising and strained muscles for both dog and owner. Cuts and abrasions should be kept clean and allowed to air-dry. Antibiotic ointment may be applied sparingly to the affected skin. Tissue and muscle soreness can be treated with ASA tablets. The maximum dose for dogs is 10 mg per kg twice daily (an average Labrador Retriever, for instance, could have one 325 mg adult aspirin morning and evening). To protect against the common side-effect of gastrointestinal bleeding, ASA should always be given with food. More severe muscle or ligament damage may require treatment with anti-inflammatory medications, but these require a veterinarian's prescription.

- For dogs with sensitive digestive systems, diarrhea is a common occurrence when the bowel chemistry is disrupted by a diet change, garbage ingestion or drinking out of stagnant puddles. Prevention is the best approach; carry an adequate supply of the dog's regular food and water. A folding bowl for this purpose is an excellent addition to the day's equipment.

- Encounters with wild creatures can result in serious discomfort for your dog. The most common hazzard is biting and stinging insects. Flea sprays available from veterinarians are often effective as a deterrent for mosquitoes and other biting insects, though they wash off easily if the dog is a swimmer. For an inquisitive nose, porcupine quills are another common problem. The quills are barbed, so they resist removal and can cause infection if the tip is broken off and left under the skin. Simply pulling the quill, which has a hollow core, will cause the barbed end to inflate, making it difficult and painful to remove. So cut the end off the quill first, then tug firmly and gently to dislodge the offender. The site should then be cleaned with hydrogen peroxide and watched closely for any sign of swelling or irritation. Rattlesnake strikes are extremely dangerous for a dog, and treatment, if possible at all, can only be performed by a veterinarian. In the unlikely event that the dog is bitten, immobilize him and seek help immediately. Avoidance is the best approach for most encounters with wildlife, so it is safest to keep the dog strictly under control, preferably on a leash.

Appendix III: Useful Contacts

The following contacts are useful general references for the excursions in this book. Contacts relating to specific excursions are listed in the Practical Information section at the end of each chapter.

Ontario Tourism
1-800-ONTARIO (668-2746)
www.ontariotravel.net
www.tourism.gov.on.ca

Ontario Parks (annual provincial parks guide and provincial park campground reservations)
1-888-668-7275
www.ontarioparks.com

Parks Canada (national parks information and campground reservations)
1-888-773-8888
www.parkscanada.gc.ca

Ontario Private Campground Association (information about privately run campgrounds)
(519) 371-3393
www.campgrounds.org

Ontario Recreational Canoeing Association (provincial paddling information)
(416) 426-7016
www.orca.on.ca

Canadian Recreational Canoeing Association (national paddling information & Kanawa magazine)
(613) 269-2910
www.paddlingcanada.com

Hike Ontario (provincial hiking association)
1-800-894-7249 or (905) 833-1787
www.hikeontario.com

Voyageur Trail Association (northern Ontario hiking)
1-877-393-4003
www3.sympatico.ca/voyageur.trail

Rideau Trail Association (eastern Ontario hiking)
(613) 545-0823
www.rideautrail.org

Ganaraska Trail Association (south-central Ontario hiking)
www3.sympatico.ca/hikers.net/ganarask.htm

Chrismar Mapping Services (Adventure Map series of topographic maps)
(905) 852-6151
www.adventuremap.com

Natural Resources Canada Centre for Topographic Information (basic information about topographic maps and links to map dealers)
1-800-465-6277
maps.nrcan.gc.ca/maps101

Ontario Nature (provincial nature association and ON Nature magazine)
1-800-440-2366 or (416) 444-8419
www.ontarionature.org

Mines and Minerals Information Centre, Ministry of Natural Resources (information, publications and maps related to the province's geology)
900 Bay Street, Toronto
1-800-665-4480

Environment Canada (weather information and forecasts)
weatheroffice.ec.gc.ca

Index

Achray – 10, 47-56
acid rain – 73, 136, 139, 152-153
Agawa Rock – 42, 43, 44, 45, 168, 169, 170, 171, 173
Algonquin Provincial Park – 10, 47, 48, 81-99, 136
Baker Homestead – 117, 118, 119
Bald Head – 174, 175, 176, 177
Barclay Estate – 82, 85, 87, 88
Barron Canyon – 47, 48-51
Berm Lake Trail – 48, 49, 51, 52, 53, 55
black rat snake – 23-24
Bon Echo Provincial Park – 10, 12, 33-41, 42, 44, 45
Bonnie's Pond Trail – 65, 66, 67, 68, 69
Booth's Rock – 84, 85, 86, 87, 88
boreal forest – 18, 57, 161, 165
Brandy Falls – 110, 111, 112
Brûlé, Étienne – 183, 187
Brush Lakes Lookout – 154, 159, 161
Calhoun Lodge – 117, 118, 119, 120
Canadian Recreational Canoeing Association – 29, 207
Carcajou Bay – 51, 52, 53, 54, 56
Centennial Ridges Trail – 88, 89, 90, 91
Chikanishing Trail – 145, 146, 148
Clifftop Trail – 35, 36, 37, 38
coniferous – 16, 17, 47, 57-61, 81
Crack, The – 137, 138, 139, 140, 141
deciduous – 16, 17, 23, 81
Devil's Chair – 177, 179, 180, 181, 182
Devil's Frying Pan – 181, 182, 183
Devil's Warehouse – 177, 179, 180, 182
diabase – 15, 115, 137, 171
dogs – 116, 171, 203-207
Eagle's Nest – 59, 70
Eastern Pines Backpacking Trail – 51, 54, 55
Eels Creek – 73, 74, 75, 77, 78, 79
fault, geological – 33, 49, 106, 110, 129, 146, 165, 177, 186
fire tower – 92, 95, 101, 113, 143, 157, 158
Flagpole Hill – 24, 26, 28
Frontenac Provincial Park – 10, 15, 23-31
Frontenac Axis – 14, 23, 33, 57
Frost Centre, The – 10, 101-113
fur trade – 19, 20, 82,146, 166, 178, 181
Gargantua – 177, 178, 179, 180, 181, 182
geology – 13, 14, 15, 23, 33, 63, 115, 135, 155, 165
geomorphology – 103, 105, 106, 107,108, 110
glaciers – 16, 23, 33, 47, 49, 63, 106, 107, 108, 115, 121, 129, 135, 155, 157, 184, 185
gneiss – 15, 115
granite – 15, 115, 135, 137, 138, 145, 147
Grenville Province – 14, 15, 23, 63, 115, 135
Group of Seven – 34, 52, 81, 135
Grundy Lake Provincial Park – 10, 127-133
Gut Lake Trail – 128, 129, 131
Hastings Heritage Trail - 70
High Falls (Achray) – 46, 51, 52, 53
High Falls (Eels Creek) – 72, 74, 75, 76, 77
Killarney Provincial Park – 8, 10, 13, 14, 15, 58, 61, 135-153
La Cloche Silhouette Trail – 137, 138, 142, 149

Lakeshore Trail – 65, 66, 67, 69, 71
Lake Superior Provincial Park – 10, 13, 15, 165-192
lamprey – 21, 148
logging – 20, 21, 25, 50, 51, 60, 64, 69, 81, 82, 94, 96, 99, 101, 136, 148, 144, 146, 157
Madawaska River – 87, 88, 89, 90, 92, 95, 96, 97
marble – 15, 23, 73
Massasauga Provincial Park, The – 10, 115-125
Massasauga rattlesnake – 115, 116, 125
Mazinaw Rock – 32, 33, 34, 35, 36, 39, 42, 45
McKenzie Backpacking Trail – 154, 159, 160, 161, 162
Midcontinental Rift – 14, 15, 165, 177
mining – 20, 63, 64, 70, 73, 133, 207
Mink Lake Lookout – 25, 28
Mishepeshu – 33, 44, 45, 166, 171
Mississagi Provincial Park – 10, 14, 15,18, 155-163
Nanabosho – 44, 166, 181, 186
Native people(s) – 19, 33, 42, 44, 45, 73, 76, 104, 166, 170, 171, 178, 180, 187
natural succession – 67, 69
Nokomis – 183, 184, 185, 186
Old Baldy – 155, 156, 157, 158
Old Woman Bay – 183, 184, 185, 186, 187, 189, 191
Orphan Lake Trail – 174, 175, 176, 177
peat – 107, 161
pegmatitie – 107, 115, 121
Petroglyphs Provincial Park – 10, 73-79
petroglyphs – 42-45, 73, 74, 76
pictographs – 33, 39, 41, 42-45, 53, 54, 87, 166, 168, 170, 171, 173
pine trees – 17, 20, 47, 57-61, 67, 81, 101, 127
Pukaskwa pits – 183, 185, 187
quartzite – 15, 135, 137, 138, 140, 141, 144, 155, 158
railway – 20, 52, 81, 82, 85, 87, 88, 89, 92, 93, 94, 95, 96
rainshadow – 47
raised cobble beach – 184, 187, 190
Raven's Cliff – 100, 102, 104, 110
Red Rock lighthouse – 145, 147, 149
Rideau Trail – 26, 29, 207
ripple-rock - 156
Science North - 133
Silent Lake Provincial Park – 10, 57, 59, 63-71
Silver Peak – 141, 142, 143, 144
Sinclair Cove – 168, 169, 170, 171
Slide Lake – 24, 25, 26, 27, 28
Southern Province – 14, 15, 23, 63, 135, 155
Stag Lake Peatland – 159, 160, 161
Superior Province – 13, 14, 155, 165
talus – 49, 166, 168, 171, 172, 173
Tarvat Bay Trail – 145, 147, 148, 151
Track & Tower Trail – 92, 93, 95, 97
Voyageur Trail – 163, 187, 188, 190, 207
Whitman, Walt – 34, 35, 39
wolf howl - 82
Wreck Island – 120, 121, 122, 124